DECADES OF THE
20TH
CENTURY

1940s

ELDORADO INK

DECADES OF THE 20TH CENTURY

1900s

1910s

1920s

1930s

1940s

1950s

1960s

1970s

1980s

1990s

DECADES OF THE
20ᵀᴴ CENTURY

1940s

ELDORADO INK

Published by Eldorado Ink
2099 Lost Oak Trail
Prescott, AZ 86303
www.eldoradoink.com

Milan Bobek, Editor
Judith C. Callomon, Historical consultant
Samuel J. Patti, Consulting editor

Printed and bound in Slovenia

Publisher Cataloging Data
1940s / [Milan Bobek, editor].
        p. cm. -- (Decades of the 20th century)
        Includes index.
        Summary: This volume, arranged chronologically, presents
key events that have shaped the decade, from significant political
occurrences to details of daily life.
        ISBN 1-932904-04-2
        1. Nineteen forties   2. History, Modern--20th century--
Chronology   3. History, Modern--20th century--Pictorial works
4. World War, 1939-1945--Pictorial works   I. Bobek, Milan
II. Title: Nineteen forties   III. Series
        909.82/4--dc22

Picture research and photography by Anne Hobart Lang and Rolf
Lang of AHL Archives. Additional research by Heritage Picture
Collection, London.

CONTENTS

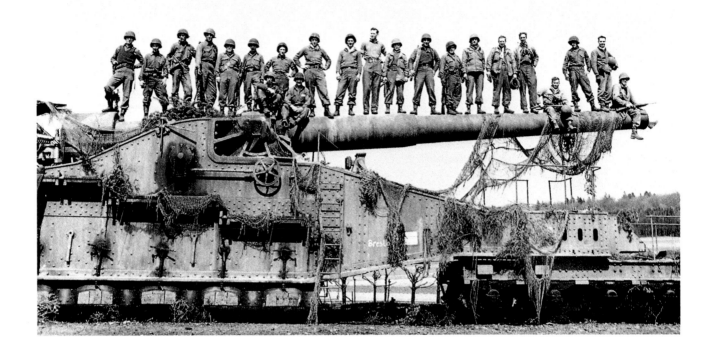

6   **1940–1949 WAR AND PEACE**
7   **1940** THE DARKEST HOUR FOR THE
          ALLIES
10 **1941** THE U.S.A. JOINS IN THE FIGHT
24 **1942** CONFLICT GOES GLOBAL: AFRICA
          AND THE FAR EAST
28 **1943** THE TIDE TURNS AS THE ALLIES
          FIGHT BACK
32 **1944** INVASION, LIBERATION, AND
          RETALIATION
36 **1945** AFTERMATH AND ATOMIC BOMBS
42 **1946** THE IRON CURTAIN COMES DOWN
46 **1947** NEW COUNTRIES AND A BABY
          BOOM
52 **1948** BERLIN BLOCKADE AND A NEW
          ISRAEL
58 **1949** NATO AND THE PEOPLE'S REPUBLIC

**WINNERS AND ACHIEVERS
OF THE DECADE**
62 ACADEMY AWARD WINNERS
62 NOBEL PRIZE WINNERS
62 INDIANAPOLIS 500 WINNERS
62 OLYMPIC SITES
62 U.S. PRESIDENTS
62 KENTUCKY DERBY WINNERS
62 NBA CHAMPIONS
62 WORLD SERIES CHAMPIONS

63 INDEX

WAR AND PEACE

America joins in the war after Pearl Harbor is attacked and warfare goes global, dominating the first half of the decade. The dropping of the atomic bomb on Hiroshima ends the war in the East, but the frightening power unleashed leads to the Campaign for Nuclear Disarmament. The Iron Curtain descends, separating East from West, and NATO is established in an effort to avoid further conflict. A spontaneous, life-affirming "baby boom" brightens the immediate post- war period as people look forward to the future.

1940–1949

KEY EVENTS OF THE DECADE

- PENICILLIN DEVELOPED
- PEARL HARBOR
- COLOR TELEVISION
- ARAB LEAGUE
- WORLD WAR II ENDS
- UNITED NATIONS
- HIROSHIMA
- IRON CURTAIN
- ATOMIC POWER

- THE NEW LOOK
- THE BABY BOOM
- MARSHALL PLAN
- PARTITION OF INDIA
- GANDHI ASSASSINATED
- STATE OF ISRAEL FOUNDED
- NATO FORMED
- PEOPLE'S REPUBLIC OF CHINA FOUNDED

WORLD POPULATION: 2,295 MILLION

THE DARKEST HOUR FOR THE ALLIES

A desperate year; as the war escalates, Holland, Belgium, and France fall in rapid succession and Britain stands temporarily alone. Allied troops are snatched from death on the beaches of Dunkirk. Winston Churchill takes over as prime minister and the Battle of Britain is fought between the Luftwaffe and the RAF in the skies over England. General de Gaulle escapes to England to rally French resistance. In Poland, the Jewish population is forced into the Warsaw Ghetto. Leo Trotsky is assassinated. One of the few gleams of light relief is Charlie Chaplin's portrayal of an absurd mustachioed megalomaniac in his film *The Great Dictator*.

1 9 4 0

Mar	12	War between Finland and Russia ends
Apr	9	Denmark falls to Germany
	14	The Toronto Maple Leafs defeat the New York Rangers to win the Stanley Cup
May	10	Winston Churchill becomes prime minister of Great Britain
	10	The Netherlands are hit by a Blitzkrieg of German airplanes in advance of troop invasions
	28	Belgium falls to Hitler
June	4	Allied troops are evacuated from Dunkirk
	10	Italy declares war on the Allies
	14	German troops march through Paris after the French military retreats

June	18	Charles de Gaulle escapes to England
	23	France surrenders
	29	Paul Klee has died of a heart attack at the age of 61
Aug	21	Leon Trotsky is assassinated with an ax in Mexico
Sep	27	Japan makes formal alliance with Italy and Germany
Oct	15	Chaplin's film *The Great Dictator* is released
	28	Italy invades Greece
	29	The first number in America's military draft lottery is drawn
Nov	5	President Roosevelt is reelected for a record third term

END OF THE WINTER WAR

A truce between the Soviet Union and Finland ends the winter war between the two countries. Finland loses some border regions to the Soviet Union in the peace treaty. The war reveals considerable weaknesses in the Red Army.

CHURCHILL TAKES THE HELM

Winston Churchill becomes prime minister of Great Britain after the fall of Neville Chamberlain. Churchill forms an all-party coalition government with the Labour party leader, Clement Attlee, as deputy prime minister.

UNDERGROUND ART

On September 12, four young men discover the painted cave at Lascaux, in southwestern France; the paintings are 17,000 years old.

FRANCE FALLS

German armies sweep into France after their successful conquest of the Netherlands and Belgium. The French government falls and a new government, led from Vichy by Marshal Henri Pétain, hero of the defense of Verdun in World War I, takes power as president and prime minister. Free French forces rally in exile in London under General Charles de Gaulle.

GAMES OFF

The Winter and Summer Olympics are canceled because of the war.

ABOVE: Hitler takes Paris and is photographed against its most enduring symbol.

LEON TROTSKY (LEV DAVIDOVICH BRONSTEIN) (1879–1940)

The Russian revolutionary has been murdered with an ice ax in Mexico City. After the Revolution, Trotsky became commissar for foreign affairs. Then as commissar for war, he recruited the Red Army to defeat the White Russians. On Lenin's death his fortunes changed, and his belief in the permanent revolution was much opposed by Stalin, who exiled him in 1929. Many years later, under glasnost, it will be revealed that he was assassinated by the secret police who were acting under Stalin's orders.

NEW DALAI LAMA

Five year old Llhamo Thondup is declared the thirteenth Dalai Lama. He is named Tenzing Gyatso and sent to study at the Tibetan monastery of Kumbum.

BLITZKRIEG

German bombers begin to attack London, concentrating on the docks in the East End. The Blitz causes many casualties. People are forced to seek shelter in subway tunnels as their homes are attacked and burned. Other major British cities, notably Plymouth and Coventry, suffer from extensive bombing.

PALAZZO DELLA CIVILITA DEL LAVORO

Mussolini plans a showcase exhibition project for 1942, Exposizione Universale di Roma. It's intended to glorify Fascism, but the idea is abandoned. One building, however, the "Palace of the Civilization of Work," is completed. Its arched facade, recalling ancient Roman architecture, becomes a symbol of the art of Fascist imperialism.

FOR WHOM THE BELL TOLLS

One of the most successful of the many literary accounts of the Spanish Civil War, Ernest Hemingway's novel deals with the relationship between a young American volunteer and a group of Republican guerrillas operating behind Franco's lines. Many say that it is his best book.

FRANCIS SCOTT (F. SCOTT) FITZGERALD (1896–1940)

The American writer has died of a heart attack at the early age of 44, still working on his book *The Last Tycoon*. His novels of the 1920s and 1930s express the mood of the "Jazz generation" who had been young during World War I. Among the best known are *The Great Gatsby* (1925) and *Tender is the Night* (1934).

AFRICAN PARK

The Serengeti, East Africa's first national park, is founded in 1929 in Tanzania. The British administrators add 900 square miles to the lion sanctuary, which now encompasses the Ngorongoro volcano crater, and makes room for an enlarged list of protected species.

PENICILLIN IS DEVELOPED

Australian-born pathologist Howard Florey and German-born chemist Ernst Chain, working in Oxford, develop penicillin as an antibiotic. It goes into mass production in the United States.

COELIAC DISEASE

Dutch doctors recognize that coeliac disease, in which the small intestine fails to absorb food, particularly fats, can be caused by sensitivity to gluten, which is the major protein of wheat and rye. This discovery comes about fortuitously when the occupying German forces requisition all supplies of wheat and rye flour, after which coeliac patients in Dutch hospitals begin to show improvement.

COLOR TELEVISION

The first daily transmission of color T.V. begins in the United States, with rotating color filters in the cameras and in the receivers.

RH FACTOR DISCOVERED

American scientists Karl Landsteiner and Philip Levine discover the Rh factor in blood. It is an antigen which can cause harm to newborn babies.

WHO IS ADENOID HYNKEL?

This is the name given by Charlie Chaplin to the protagonist of his film *The Great Dictator*, mocking the activities of Hitler and Mussolini.

ABOVE: Winston Churchill leads the British Conservative party following the death of Chamberlain.

ABOVE: Erwin Rommel, one of Hitler's leading commanders, successfully leads a panzer division during the invasion of France in 1940 and is later appointed commander of the Afrika Korps.

TWO MORE ELEMENTS

U.S. physicists Edwin M. McMillan and Philip H. Abelson discover the element neptunium, with an atomic number of 93; McMillan, Glenn T. Seaborg and others then discover plutonium, atomic number 94.

GPV SPELLS JEEP

The U.S. Army test-runs a prototype all-terrain reconnaissance vehicle, the GPV or General Purpose Vehicle. Later, this acronym will be shortened to jeep.

BIG MACS START SMALL

Movie theater owners Richard and Maurice McDonald set up their first hamburger stand, a drive-in near Pasadena, California.

(ARTHUR) NEVILLE CHAMBERLAIN (1869–1940)

The former British prime minister has died, six months after being replaced by Winston Churchill. He will go down in history waving the Munich Agreement of 1938 and saying "Peace in our time" as he returns from yielding to Hitler's claim for Sudetenland (in Czechoslovakia) in exchange for peace.

THE U.S.A. JOINS IN THE FIGHT

Franklin D. Roosevelt introduces Lend-Lease, without which, the Allies would likely lose the war. This is not popular with isolationists in the United States, but attitudes change when Japan strikes home, devastating the U.S. Pacific Fleet at Pearl Harbor, Hawaii. America enters the war in earnest. Hitler invades Russia. Civilian populations on both sides suffer from heavy bombing raids on cities and towns. Jet aircraft enter the fray on both sides and the world is introduced to Spam, the taste of wartime.

1941

Mar	28	English author Virginia Woolf commits suicide by drowning herself at the age of 58
Apr	17	German forces have captured the Yugoslavian capital of Belgrade
May	27	The *Bismarck* sinks
June	1	Greece falls to Germany
Aug	14	Churchill and Roosevelt meet to sign the Atlantic Charter
Sep	19	Germany takes Kiev and breaks the Nazi-Soviet Non-Aggression Pact
Nov	1	Mt. Rushmore with its portraits of U.S. presidents is unveiled
Dec	7	Pearl Harbor is bombed

LEND-LEASE
The Lend-Lease Bill becomes law, allowing the U.S. president to sell, lend or lease material to countries whose defense is important to the United States. Britain benefits hugely from this, granting 99 year, rent-free leases for naval bases in the Caribbean and Newfoundland to the United States in return for 50 destroyers.

U.S.S.R. AND JAPAN MAKE A PACT
The U.S.S.R. signs a neutrality pact with Japan, which lasts until the final days of the war in 1945. The pact ensures that both Japan and the U.S.S.R. do not have to fight on two fronts. It frees up the U.S.S.R. to fight Germany and Japan can now attack the United States and Southeast Asia.

LONDON DEVASTATED
The heaviest German bombing raid of the war hits London, with 550 bombers dropping 100,000 incendiaries and numerous bombs on the capital. The House of Commons is destroyed and more than 1,400 people are killed. More than 20,000 people have been killed in London and 25,000 injured, since German bombers began hitting the city.

SHELTER ART
English sculptor Henry Moore (1898–1986) produces a series of drawings of people in London's air-raid shelters. Images of ordinary people coping in a crisis are some of the most poignant pictures of the war. They are also highly sculptural, fine examples of how a sculptor can capture the mass and form of figures in a drawing.

ABOVE: The U.S. base at Pearl Harbor is attacked unexpectedly at dawn by some 360 Japanese aircraft.

PEARL HARBOR

Following the Japanese attack on the U.S. fleet in Pearl Harbor in the Pacific Ocean, the United States enters the war. The U.S. economy is put on a war footing, with factories turned over to war production and thousands of women pressed into factory work.

YELLOW STAR

The infamous yellow Star of David is imposed on German Jews over the age of six to make them easily recognizable. Jews in Poland already wear such a star.

AMY JOHNSON
(1903–1941)

The English pioneer aviator has been lost in a plane accident while on active service in the British Air Transport Auxiliary. She was the first woman to fly solo from England to Australia in 1930. She also made several record solo flights, as well as flying across the Atlantic with her husband, James Mollison, in 1933 and with him to India in 1934.

CITIZEN KANE

A triumph for Orson Welles (although initially it does not do well at the box office), this film charts the life of a newspaper magnate based on William Randolph Hearst. Welles co-writes, produces, directs, and stars. He is established as a Hollywood prodigy, combining camerawork, music, narrative technique, and lighting to produce one of the most impressive films ever.

ATLANTIC CHARTER

British prime minister Winston Churchill and President Franklin D. Roosevelt meet on board a warship off the Newfoundland coast and agree to the Atlantic Charter, which ties the two countries closely together.

TWIN-ENGINED JET FIGHTER . . .

The world's first twin-engined fighter aircraft, the German Heinkel He 280, makes its first flight in April. However, it does not go into production.

. . . AND FIRST BRITISH JET

In May, the Gloster E-28/3 experimental aircraft, using one of Frank Whittle's jet engines, makes its maiden flight. It goes into production in 1944 and is named the Gloster Meteor.

JAMES AUGUSTINE ALOYSIUS JOYCE
(1882–1941)

The influential Irish writer has died in Zurich after an operation for a duodenal ulcer. Since 1902, he has lived mainly in Europe, principally in Paris, where the "stream of consciousness" novel *Ulysses* was published in 1922. *The Dubliners* (1914), *A Portrait of the Artist as a Young Man* (1914-15), and *Finnegans Wake* (1939) are among his other works.

SYMPHONY FOR LENINGRAD

The first three movements of Dmitri Shostakovich's Symphony No. 7 are written while the city is being bombarded. The music is performed with the echoes of bombs in the background. It becomes a work that is closely identified with the heroic Russian role in World War II.

LET US NOW PRAISE FAMOUS MEN

American photographer Walker Evans (1903–1975) had worked with writer and journalist James Agee (1909–1965) in the late 1930s, taking photographs in Alabama to go with Agee's text about the Depression in the South. The intention was to produce an article for *Fortune* magazine, but it was not used. Agee decided to expanded the text and the result is this landmark book.

MOTHER COURAGE

German dramatist Bertolt Brecht's great play is first performed in Zurich. It is a complex play, in which Brecht tries to show that war makes us, including Mother Courage herself, inhuman. But audiences respond positively to the vitality of the main character and Brecht changes the text after this performance.

BUG SPRAYS

Insecticides in aerosol cans are supplied to U.S. troops in the Pacific. These "bug bombs," using freon gas, were developed by research chemist L.D. Goodhue and entomologist W.N. Sullivan as a protection against insect-borne diseases. The aerosol can was invented in Norway in 1926.

SPAM, SPAM, SPAM

Spam, a tinned processed meat made mainly from pork, becomes a wartime staple for troops and civilians.

BELOW: In the New York Yankees squad are (left to right) Joe DiMaggio, Charles (King Kong) Keller, and Bill Dickey.

ABOVE: The powerful beams of antiaircraft lights lace the night sky.

(ADELINE) VIRGINIA WOOLF (née STEPHEN) (1882–1941)

The English experimental writer and modernist has committed suicide. Having long suffered from bouts of depression, she was found drowned in the Ouse River near her home in Sussex. Her works include *Mrs. Dalloway* (1925), *To the Lighthouse* (1927), and the feminist essay *A Room of One's Own* (1929). She and her husband Leonard Woolf founded the Hogarth Press, publisher of T.S. Eliot, in 1917 and her name is synonymous with the Bloomsbury Group.

THE DESERT FOX
Germany's General Erwin Rommel "the Desert Fox" and his Africa Korps have landed in Libya to reverse recent Italian setbacks.

FIRST POLYESTER FIBER
J.R. Whitfield and J.T. Dickson, scientists working for the British Calico Printer's Association, make the first polyester textile fiber. It is later marketed under the names of Terylene™ and Dacron™.

COLD COMFORT
Freeze-dried orange juice is supplied to the U.S. army after freeze-drying is adapted for the preservation of foods and drinks in the United States. Frozen food or drink, dried in a heated chamber, can be reconstituted quickly without loss of flavor.

DIGNIFIED IN STONE
The Mount Rushmore National Memorial is unveiled. The granite faces of presidents Lincoln, Washington, Jefferson, and Roosevelt survey the Black Hills of South Dakota. The work was begun 15 years previously by sculptor Gutzon Borglum, who died before seeing his masterpiece completed.

WORLD WAR II

The greatest conflict of the twentieth century, World War II, touches every continent and devastates some. The best estimate for casualties is 15 million military dead and 25 million military wounded. Civilian deaths are about 38 million. Huge parts of the European and Russian infrastructure are destroyed and the populations of Eastern European states are displaced as national borders are adjusted.

❖KEY DATES❖
WORLD WAR II

March 12, 1938 AUSTRIA ANNEXED German troops enter Austria to ensure *Anschluss* (union) with Germany.

March 15, 1939 CZECHOSLOVAKIA German troops enter Prague and Czechoslovakia is dismantled.

Sept 1–Oct 7, 1939 POLAND Poland is crushed by armored and mechanized forces backed by bombers and fighter ground attack aircraft. German casualties are 14,000 killed and 30,300 wounded, while Polish casualties are believed to exceed 120,000 plus 450,000 prisoners.

Sept 3, 1939 BRITAIN Britain declares war on Germany.

April 9, 1940 DENMARK The tiny country is seized by the Germans to give them airfields for the attack on Norway.

April 9–June 8, 1940 NORWAY The German invasion of Norway, intended to protect supplies of iron ore from Sweden, cost the Germans 5,300 killed or wounded, three cruisers, ten destroyers, eight submarines, 11 transports, and 11 other ships.

May 10–June 25, 1940 HOLLAND The Germans attack in the west. This draws British and French troops into Holland before the Germans break through at Sedan and in a drive to the channel, they cut the British off from France. Holland falls on May 15 and Belgium on May 27. France capitulates on June 22 and hostilities end on June 25. On the ground, Germany suffers 27,000 killed, 110,000 wounded and 18,000 missing. France loses 90,000 dead, 200,000 wounded, and 1.9 million are either taken prisoner or missing. The Belgians have 23,000 casualties and the Dutch 10,000. Britain loses 68,000 casualties. In the air, the Luftwaffe lose 1,284 aircraft, the RAF 931, and the French 560.

ABOVE: A mass roll-call of SA, SS, and NSKK troops in Nuremberg. During the first year of the war, Germany has the manpower, equipment, and will to win that gives her a great advantage.

DUNKIRK EVACUATION

German tank divisions trap British, French, and Belgian troops around the port of Dunkirk on the north coast of France. Between May 26 and June 4, 1940, in one of the most dramatic events of the war, 338,000 soldiers are rescued by the Royal Navy with assistance from the French and many civilian vessels from England.

ABOVE: Nazis rally in Nuremberg.

BELOW: Hitler announces the annexation of Austria to an ecstatic Reichstag.

RIGHT: A Czech woman's grief-stricken submission as Germany annexes Czechoslovakia, in one of many expansionist actions towards the east.

THEATERS OF WAR

NORTH AFRICA AND THE MEDITERRANEAN 1940–1943

The campaign in North Africa fought by the British with United States' assistance in late 1942 against the Italians and Germans (Axis Powers), is unique in World War II. The theater has few civilians, so casualties are confined to the armies and the tactics developed for the desert are similar to those employed in naval warfare.

TOBRUK
Jan 22–Nov, 1941 and June 18–June 20, 1942

The former Italian port is held by British and Commonwealth forces behind German lines from January to November 1941. However, when it is again besieged by the Germans in June 1942, they press their attacks home and this time the port is captured with valuable supplies and 33,000 prisoners.

EL ALAMEIN Oct 23–Nov 4, 1942

The British and Commonwealth attack the Axis forces, who are well dug in. The British losses are 2,350 killed and 8,950 wounded, with 2,260 missing. The Axis losses are 10,000 killed, 15,000 wounded, and 30,000 captured.

"TORCH" LANDINGS
Nov 8, 1942

Some 36,000 British and American forces land in two locations in French Northwest Africa, in effect squeezing Axis forces from the west.

YUGOSLAVIA AND GREECE
April 6–April 23, 1941

After the Italian Army becomes embroiled in Greece and Yugoslavia launches a coup against its pro-Axis government, Hitler decides to invade Yugoslavia and Greece. German casualties in Yugoslavia are 558 while 345,000 Yugoslavian soldiers are captured. In Greece, the Germans have 4,500 casualties. Greek losses are 70,000 killed or wounded and 270,000 captured. British forces assisting the Greeks suffer 12,000 casualties.

OPERATION "MERCURY" May 20, 1941

German airborne assault on Crete. The Luftwaffe lands 22,750 men using 493 Ju 52 transport aircraft and about 80 gliders. Though it is a German victory, 4,500 of their men are killed and 150 transport aircraft lost.

ABOVE: General Montgomery's determination overcame Field Marshal Rommel's Afrika Korps.

LEFT: Russians break through German defenses outside Leningrad.

SOVIET UNION AND EASTERN FRONT 1941–1944

Hitler boasts that the Soviet Union is so decrepit that "We have only to kick in the door and the whole rotten structure will come crashing down." He plans to deport or execute their high-ranking officials.

MINSK June–July, 1941
A battle of encirclement is fought in which 15 Soviet divisions are destroyed.

SIEGE OF LENINGRAD
Sept 1, 1941–Jan 27, 1944
Besieged for almost the duration of the war, Leningrad withstands German attacks. By 1944 nearly one million of its inhabitants have been killed or starved to death.

KHARKOV Oct 24, 1941–Aug 22, 1943
The scene of heavy fighting in 1942 and 1943, Kharkov is the location for a major battle of encirclement in which 250,000 Soviet prisoners are taken in 1942.

SEVASTOPOL Nov 1941–July 3, 1942
The Black Sea port and Soviet naval base is besieged by ten German infantry divisions with 120 batteries of artillery. The Soviet forces number 106,000 men with 700 guns and mortars. Though the port is captured, some defenders are evacuated by small boats.

STALINGRAD Aug 19, 1942–Jan 31, 1943
The attack on the Russian city is a disaster for Hitler, leading to the defeat of the German 6th Army and the loss of 1.5 million men, 3,500 tanks, 12,000 guns and mortars, 75,000 vehicles, and 3,000 aircraft.

KURSK July 5–July 17, 1943
This is the German counteroffensive, of which the Russians are well aware through signals intelligence. In the fighting, both sides lose over 1,500 tanks, but the Russians swing on to the offensive and the Germans lose the initiative for good.

BERLIN April 16–May 2, 1945
The final battle for the German capital costs the Russians 100,000 killed, while 136,000 prisoners are taken. It is estimated that 100,000 civilians are killed in the fighting.

WARSAW UPRISING

Between August 1 and October 2, 1944, Polish patriots rise to liberate their city from German occupation as the Soviet army approaches. However, on Stalin's orders, they halt until the Poles have been defeated.

ABOVE: A massive bombardment is launched at Monte Cassino.

SICILY AND ITALY 1943–1945

Churchill proposes that Italy should be attacked since he describes it as "the soft underbelly" of the Axis. It proves to be a much tougher undertaking than imagined, involving amphibious operations and fighting in mountains in bitter winter weather.

SICILY July 10–Aug 18, 1943
Landings by British and American forces push the Axis towards the Strait of Messina. They are able to evacuate 40,000 Germans and 60,000 Italians but suffer 178,000 casualties and captured. Allied casualties are 31,158 including 11,923 Americans.

SALERNO Sept 9, 1943
The landing on the mainland of Italy by U.S. and British forces is vigorously counterattacked by the Germans. Only after reinforcements have been rushed in does it become secure. On September 15, the Germans begin to pull back.

ANZIO Jan 22–May 25, 1944
An amphibious operation intended to outflank Cassino, the Anzio attack becomes in effect stuck on the beaches where the U.S. forces suffer 21,000 casualties and the Germans about 11,000.

MONTE CASSINO Feb 15–May 18, 1944
This strong defensive position costs the Allies 21,000 casualties including 4,100 killed in action. When Cassino falls, the Allies take 20,000 prisoners and open the road to Rome.

ROME June 5, 1944
Liberated by the Americans, the drive on the Italian capital city actually allows the German 10th Army to escape as a formed unit.

THE FIGHT FOR EUROPE

NORMANDY AND NORTHWEST EUROPE 1942–1945

BRUNEVAL Feb 27–28, 1942

In a combined operation, a company of British paratroops launches a raid against a German radar station and an RAF technician removes key components before the force is evacuated by the Royal Navy.

DIEPPE Aug 19, 1942

A large-scale raid against the French port of Dieppe by 5,000 Canadians and 1,000 Commandos is almost a complete disaster. The Canadians lose 215 officers and 3,164 men, the Commandos 24 officers and 223 men, while German losses are 345 killed and 268 wounded.

COUTANCES
July 17, 1944

USAF P-38 Lightnings are involved in the first napalm attack in Normandy launched against a fuel depot at Coutances.

FALAISE POCKET
Aug 13–21, 1944

The German forces trapped by the United States break out at St. Lo and are pounded from the air. When the pocket closes, only 20,000 out of the 80,000 trapped Germans escape. They leave behind vast amounts of weapons and equipment.

ARNHEM
Sept 17–25, 1944

The Arnhem operation is part of an airborne attack to capture bridges across the lower Rhine. British forces from the 1st Airborne Division are forced to withdraw after heavy German attacks. British losses are 1,130 killed and 6,000 captured, of whom half are wounded.

BELOW: The Allied raid on Dieppe costs the lives of thousands of Canadian troops.

D-DAY JUNE 6, 1944

The Anglo-American landings on the Normandy coast turn the tide of the war in Europe. They involve 1,213 warships, 4,126 landing ships, 736 ancillary vessels, and 864 merchant vessels. By midnight on June 6, 57,500 American and 75,000 British and Canadian forces are ashore. The Allied casualties are 2,500 killed and 8,500 wounded.

ABOVE: Arnhem's sky blossoms with British paratroopers as the disastrous Operation Market Garden begins.

ARDENNES
Dec 16,1944–Jan 16, 1945

The last great German offensive in the West has initial successes against the U.S. Army, but is halted and destroyed by U.S. forces with some British help. Losses are 100,000 German casualties, 81,000 American, and 1,400 British.

REMAGEN
March 7, 1945

The Ludendorf railroad bridge across the Rhine is captured intact by men of the U.S. 9th Armored Division.

RHINE CROSSINGS
March 23, 1945

Full-scale amphibious crossings and airborne landings put British and U.S. forces in a position to capture the industrial heartland of the Ruhr.

WAR IN THE EAST 1941–1945

Although Japan has been involved in China, its war with the United States and Britain does not begin until December 1941. The Japanese hope that through tactical success at Pearl Harbor they will be able to access oil, raw material supplies, and territorial assets.

HONG KONG Dec 8–25, 1941
Despite being outnumbered and outgunned, the British put up a stout defense. Casualties are 2,000 with 11,000 prisoners; the Japanese lose 2,745 killed.

MALAYSIA AND SINGAPORE
Dec 8, 1941–Feb 15, 1942
The British fight a series of delaying actions down the Malay Peninsula, suffering 5,000 casualties, following Japanese landings in three locations. The Japanese capture Singapore with 9,800 casualties. They take 32,000 Indian, 16,000 British, and 14,000 Australian prisoners, more than 50 percent of whom are to die in captivity.

PHILIPPINES Dec 10, 1941–May 6–7, 1942
Japanese troops land on the Philippines and push the American and Filipino soldiers back to the Bataan Peninsula, which they hold until April 9. Some 76,000 men surrender; however, at least 10,000 die during their march to prison. The last defenses to fall are those of Corregidor, where the garrison suffers 2,000 casualties.

NEW GUINEA Mar 7, 1942–Aug 26, 1944
Following Japanese landings, Australian and U.S. forces counterattack and, over a long campaign, defeat Japan. The cost is 57,046 Australian casualties, of whom 12,161 are killed. U.S. casualties are 19,000, while the Japanese lose 13,000 in Papua and 35,000 in New Guinea.

TARAWA Nov 20–23, 1943
Defended by 4,800 Japanese marines, Tarawa costs the U.S. Marine Corps 1,500 killed or wounded.

KOHIMA/IMPHAL, BURMA April 4–18, 1944
About 13,000 Japanese are killed in the siege of Kohima and at Imphal 53,000 perish from a combination of disease and combat. These two victories are the turning point for the British in Burma.

SAIPAN June 15–July 9, 1944
Out of a garrison of 30,000, only 1,000 Japanese prisoners are taken. U.S. casualties are 1,037 marines and 3,674 soldiers, including 3,426 dead.

GUAM July 21–Aug 10, 1944
Defended by 20,000 men, the island falls with the loss of 6,716 marines, 839 soldiers, and 245 sailors, including 1,023 dead. Its capture gives the USAF a base for heavy bomber raids on Japan.

ABOVE: Japanese forces land on the island fortress of Corregidor, overcoming a valiant stand by U.S. and Filipino troops.

IWO JIMA Feb 16–March 26, 1945
Fighting for a tiny island of eight square miles defended by 21,000 troops, the Americans suffer 6,821 dead and 18,200 wounded. There are few Japanese survivors. Iwo Jima is strategically important; it had been used as an airstrip for Japanese fighter planes, making it easy for them to attack U.S. bombers.

OKINAWA April 1–July 2, 1945
The casualties in the fighting for this 794 square mile island are 2,938 marines and 4,675 soldiers dead, with 31,807 wounded. The Japanese lose 100,000 killed and 10,000 captured.

THE PHILIPPINE CAMPAIGN

This lasts from October 17, 1944 to July 4, 1945. The liberation of the Philippine Island group is a particular concern for the U.S. commander in the Far East, General Douglas MacArthur, who has spent much of his career in the area.

LEYTE Oct 17–Dec 25, 1944
The American casualties are 15,584, including 3,584 killed. Japanese figures are not known, but are believed to be 70,000 killed.

LUZON Dec 15, 1944–July 4, 1945
Heavy fighting leads to the liberation of the island which contains the capital of the Philippines, Manila. The Americans suffer 37,854 killed or wounded, in Manila alone. Japanese losses are 16,000 killed.

CORREGIDOR Feb 16–21, 1945
The Americans launch a combined sea and airborne attack on the fortified island, where at least 3,300 Japanese perish.

AIR WAR IN THE WEST

THE BATTLE OF BRITAIN July 10–Oct 12, 1940

With the fall of France, Britain has no allies left in Western Europe. Hitler's plan is to launch air attacks against Britain as a preliminary for an invasion by German ground forces. The Luftwaffe strength is 2,800 aircraft, the RAF has 700. Nearly 500 RAF pilots are killed and 400 are wounded. Even so, Britain holds off the Luftwaffe and prevents invasion.

BLITZKRIEG Sept 7, 1940–May 10, 1941

After failure in the Battle of Britain, Hermann Goering, commander of the Luftwaffe, turns to flying by night and dropping bombs on civilian targets. Ports and big cities get the worst of it. London is hit almost every night. On November 14-15, 1940, the Midlands city of Coventry is devastated when some 449 German bombers drop 503 tons of high explosive and 881 canisters of incendiaries, killing 550 and injuring 1,200.

FIRST FLIGHT OF TWIN-ENGINED JET AIRCRAFT April 2, 1941

The German He 280 goes into action. The maximum level speed is 510 miles per hour.

THE DAMBUSTERS May 16–17, 1943

Attacks by RAF bombers using specialized "bouncing" bombs against the Sorpe, Mohne, and Eder dams are launched. Though the Mohne and Eder are breached, the Sorpe is only damaged.

PEENEMUNDE August 17-18, 1943

Following intelligence that Peenemunde on the Baltic is a rocket research center, it is attacked by RAF Lancaster bombers.

V-WEAPON CAMPAIGN
June 13, 1944–March 29, 1945

The *Vergeltungswaffen* or vengeance weapons are the V-1 (the ZZG-76 flying bomb) and the V-2 (the A-4 ballistic missile). About 35,000 V-1s are produced and 9,521 are fired at Britain, of which 4,621 are destroyed. About 5,000 V-2s are launched against London, Antwerp, and Liège. On August 4, 1944, a Gloster Meteor jet fighter downs a V-1. The pilot, Flying Officer Dean, tips the missile into the ground with his wing.

JET FIGHTERS IN ACTION Oct 1944

Me 262 jet fighters engage the USAF and RAF. The first aerial victory is a B-17 shot down by a pilot of Kommando Nowotny.

OPPOSITE: The V-2 rocket, Hitler's vengeance weapon.

RAF AND USAF BOMBING CAMPAIGN

The Royal Air Force (RAF) opens the war by dropping leaflets over Germany. By the close of the war, the United States Air Force (USAF) is attacking enemy targets by day while the RAF flies by night. Though military and economic targets are hit, the RAF also destroy huge areas of housing.

• On May 30–31, 1942, the RAF flies 1,046 bombers over Cologne where it drops 1,455 tons of bombs killing 486 people, injuring 5,027, and destroying 18,440 buildings. Between 1943 and 1944, the Ruhr, Germany's industrial heartland, is attacked by the RAF and USAF. By the end of 1943, the Allied Air Forces have dropped 200,000 tons of bombs on Germany and much of that on the Ruhr.

• On July 24, 27, 29, and August 2, 1943, incendiary attacks create a firestorm that destroys 8.5 square miles of Hamburg and kills 44,600 civilians and 800 servicemen. Between August 23, 1943 and March 1944, a series of 16 heavy raids by the RAF on Berlin damages the city, but does not prevent it working as a capital. Out of 9,111 sorties, the RAF loses 492 bombers.

• On August 17 and October 14, 1943, the USAF stages raids on the German ballbearing plants at Schweinfurt, which, though of considerable strategic value, are very costly: 36 bombers are lost in the first raid and 60 in the second.

• On February 13–14, 1945, RAF and USAF bombers kill between 30,000 and 60,000 civilians in Dresden, many of them refugees, in day and night attacks.

AIR WAR IN THE EAST

PEARL HARBOR, HAWAII Dec 7, 1941

This is the event that brings the United States into the war. In a surprise early morning attack by the Japanese, lasting no more than two hours, 135 Japanese dive bombers, 104 high-level bombers, and 81 fighter aircraft flying from carriers sink or damage 18 warships, destroy 187 aircraft, and kill 2,400 U.S. servicemen. The U.S. carriers are at sea, escape, and become the main warships in the Pacific. The Japanese lose 29 aircraft and five midget submarines.

DOOLITLE TOKYO RAID April 18, 1942

Sixteen North American B-25 Mitchells commanded by Lt. Col. James Doolittle, flying from the USS *Hornet*, attack Tokyo, Nagoya, Kobe, and Yokohama and then fly on to China.

KAMIKAZE ATTACKS Oct 19, 1944–April 1945

Attacks by about 5,000 suicide aircraft sink or damage about six major Allied ships, including an escort carrier at Leyte Gulf in the Philippines.

TOKYO FIRE RAIDS March 9–10, 1945

The first incendiary attack against the Japanese capital devastates the city center and kills 100,000 people.

HIROSHIMA Aug 6, 1945

Atomic bomb nicknamed "Little Boy" is dropped on the Japanese city by a B-29 piloted by Colonel Paul Tibbets and initiates nuclear warfare. The bomb destroys 47 square miles and kills 70,000 people.

NAGASAKI Aug 9, 1945

Atomic bomb nicknamed "Fat Man" is dropped by a B-29 piloted by Major Charles Sweeney, killing 24,000 people.

LEFT: Lt. Col. James Doolittle with one of his B-25 Mitchell bombers that carried out the Tokyo raid. He is to become the commander of the 8th Air Force in 1944 and 1945.

NAVAL WAR IN THE WEST

THE ADMIRAL GRAF SPEE
Dec 13–17, 1939

After a running battle with three British cruisers, the German pocket battleship *Admiral Graf Spee* is scuttled by her captain in the River Plate, on orders from Berlin.

TARANTO Nov 11,1940

In this naval air action, 27 Swordfish torpedo bombers from the carrier HMS *Illustrious* attack the Italian fleet, while safe in its base at Taranto. They cripple three battleships, two cruisers, and sink two other ships. The British lose two aircraft.

CAPE MATAPAN
Mar 27–28,1941

Using signal intercepts, three British battleships are able to engage three Italian 8 inch cruisers, two smaller cruisers, and two destroyers, and sink them as well as damaging a battleship. The British lose two naval aircraft.

ABOVE: The *Graf Spee*, severely damaged during the Battle of the River Plate, is scuttled by its captain.

HMS HOOD AND BISMARCK May 24–27, 1941

The *Bismarck* is one of the most powerful battleships of the war, used to attack Atlantic shipping. On May 24, 1941, it sinks the British battle cruiser HMS *Hood* off the Greenland coast. Almost the entire British Navy sets out to hunt the *Bismarck* down and finally catches her off the coast of France on May 26. It takes the combined firepower of five destroyers, two battleships, and a cruiser to sink her.

OPERATION CERBERUS, THE "CHANNEL DASH" Feb 12, 1942

The German battle cruisers *Gneisenau* and *Scharnhorst* and heavy cruiser *Prinz Eugen* make a daylight run up the Channel from Brest, France, to Germany. Both battle cruisers are damaged by British mines.

NAVAL WAR IN THE EAST

THE BATTLE OF THE CORAL SEA
May 6–8, 1942

This is the first major naval action in the world fought entirely by aircraft. The U.S. Navy loses the carrier *Lexington* and the Japanese the carrier *Shoho*. The victory prevents Japan from attacking shipping lanes to Australia.

MIDWAY June 3–6, 1942

This is the turning point of the naval war in the Pacific. The U.S. Navy sinks the Japanese heavy carrier *Akagi*, the carriers *Kaga* and *Soryu*, and later the carrier *Hiryu*. The United States loses 150 aircraft, 307 men, the destroyer *Hammann*, and the carrier *Yorktown*. Victory for the United States cripples Japanese air power and prevents Japan from taking Midway to use as a base to attack Hawaii.

THE BATTLE OF THE PHILIPPINE SEA
June 19–20, 1944

U.S. pilots down 330 Japanese aircraft, with losses of 30, in an air action called "The Great Marianas Turkey Shoot." The U.S. submarine *Albacore* sinks the carrier *Taiho* and the submarine *Cavalla* sinks the carrier *Shokaku*.

THE BATTLE FOR LEYTE GULF, PHILIPPINES
Oct 23–26, 1944

Losses are severe on both sides in a three-part naval action, the biggest ever in terms of tonnage. By the close, the U.S. Navy has lost three carriers, two destroyers, and a destroyer escort. The battle costs the Japanese three battleships, four carriers, ten cruisers, and nine destroyers. The Japanese use kamikaze planes, but victory goes to the United States.

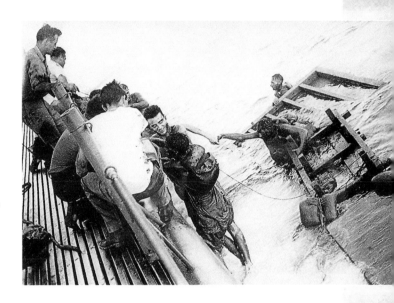

ABOVE: British and Australian survivors are rescued by the USS *Sealion*.

MUSASHI AND THE YAMATO SUNK
Oct 24 and April 7, 1945

The *Musashi* and her sister ship the *Yamato* are the largest, most heavily protected and armed battleships in the world and constitute a threat to Allied forces. They are sunk by aircraft from U.S. carriers.

ABOVE: The American navy enters Ulithi anchorage.

RIGHT: The U.S.S *Pennsylvania* and three cruisers move into Lingayen Gulf.

CONFLICT GOES GLOBAL: AFRICA AND THE FAR EAST

The Japanese take Singapore and Europe has to face fighting in the East, at the same time as establishing a front in North Africa. America avenges Pearl Harbor with a victory over the Japanese at Midway in the Pacific. In France, the collaborationist Vichy government falls. In Berlin, Hitler openly discusses the "Final Solution" to what he considers to be the Jewish problem. The forerunner of the United Nations is established. The film *Casablanca* encapsules the romance of resistance to tyranny.

1 9 4 2

Jan	1	26 nations sign the Declaration of the United Nations
Feb	15	Singapore falls to Japan
Apr	9	Troops on the Bataan Peninsula are defeated by the Japanese and the "death march" begins
May	30	The RAF pounds Cologne in a nighttime raid
June	7	Battle of Midway; U.S. avenges Pearl Harbor
Oct	23	Allies win battle of El Alamein

RIGHT: Russian air ace Col. Tashin leaves one of the bombers supplied by the United States.

ABOVE: An Allied convoy moving through Iran with supplies for Russia. The United States supplies weapons, equipment and airplanes to the Soviet Union.

LEFT: U.S. military aircraft in Alaska waiting to be ferried to Russia as part of the Lend-Lease plan.

ABOVE: A welcome halt for this U.S. supply convoy in the mountains of Iran.

THE NATIONS UNITE

The United States, Soviet Union, Britain, China, and 22 other allied nations, calling themselves the United Nations, pledge not to make separate peace treaties with Germany, Italy, or Japan. The conference in Washington forms the basis of the United Nations Organization.

ANTI-BRITISH FEELING IN INDIA

The Congress Party of India calls upon the British to "quit India" immediately. Civil disorder follows in the fall and several Congress leaders are interned.

MARTIAL MUSIC

American bandleader Glenn Miller heads up a band composed of U.S. Army personnel.

BELOW: Irving Berlin's "God Bless America" becomes the unofficial U.S. national anthem.

ABOVE: British premier Winston Churchill at a parade of Russian troops during his visit to Moscow.

THE NAZI SOLUTION

Nazi leaders meeting in secret at Wannsee discuss the "Final Solution of the Jewish Question." Plans are drawn up to exterminate all Jews in Europe in six death camps established for the purpose.

LOSING SINGAPORE

The surrender of the island fortress of Singapore to Japan marks the end of British invincibility in the Far East. The Japanese encourage revolt among the British, French, and Dutch colonies in the region and support Asian claims to independent government.

WAR IN AFRICA

As German forces continue to invade the Soviet Union, pressure grows for a second front in Western Europe against Hitler, to relieve pressure on the Red Army. Britain and the States consider invading North Africa.

MESSERSCHMITTS OUT OF THE SUN

The German Messerschmitt Me 262A-1, a twin-engined fighter, becomes the world's first jet aircraft to enter operational service.

ABOVE: In the film *Casablanca*, Humphrey Bogart and Ingrid Bergman play star-crossed lovers in a city riddled with wartime intrigue.

FIRST NUCLEAR REACTOR

Italian-born physicist Enrico Fermi (1901–1954) starts up the first nuclear reactor, built on the squash court of Chicago University. It demonstrates the first controlled chain reaction.

VICHY FALLS

German troops occupy Vichy France, ending the semi-independence of the country. The French fleet is scuttled in Toulon harbor to prevent it falling into German hands.

MILITARY CHOPPERS

The Sikorsky XR-2 becomes the first helicopter designed and built for military service and is tested by the U.S. Army.

FIRST V-2 ROCKET

On October 2, the Germans make the first successful launch of their V-2 rocket. It flies for about 12 miles and will go into active service in 1944.

FAMINE RELIEF

The charity Oxfam is founded in the U.K. as the Oxford Committee for Famine Relief, to fight world famine.

THE WARSAW GHETTO

The Germans storm the Warsaw Ghetto in September, killing its 50,000 Jewish inhabitants. The population of Polish Jews, which numbered 2.5 million in 1939, is steadily reduced as the Germans kill or transport all Jews to death camps.

OF ALL THE BARS IN ALL THE TOWNS ...

Humphrey Bogart stars as Rick, Ingrid Bergman as Ilsa, in *Casablanca*, the anti-Nazi film directed by Hungarian-born Michael Curtiz. It becomes an instant classic and combines the tension of a thriller with the element of romance.

ABOVE: Bing Crosby (left) and Bob Hope (above) continue their popular road movies; this year Morocco is the destination.

THE OUTSIDER

French novelist Albert Camus' novel about a man who cannot respond to normal conventions and social rituals becomes emblematic of a modern dilemma — how to find our own values when we reject those of the society around us. This first novel puts its author at the forefront of modern debate. His book of essays *The Myth of Sisyphus*, introducing the idea of "the Absurd", also appears this year.

ANTIGONE: A MYTH FOR TODAY

French dramatist Jean Anouilh's updating of the Greek myth enacts the troubles of contemporary France. The oppressive Creon becomes symbolic of the Vichy compromise, the idealistic Antigone with the values of freedom.

CORE SET UP

The Congress of Racial Equality (CORE) is founded by University of Chicago students led by James Farmer, to end racial segregation and discrimination in the United States by nonviolent means. John Harold Johnson begins publication of the *Negro Digest* in Chicago.

FIRST SIGHT OF A FASHION BASIC

The T-shirt appears as regulation U.S. Navy outerwear, specified as a "T-type" knitted cotton shirt, with a round neck and short sleeves set at right angles for maximum underarm sweat absorption. T-type shirts were formerly worn only as underwear.

HOT STUFF

The self-heating can is produced by Heinz to sustain hungry troops when cooking is impossible. When the cap is peeled back, a fuse ignites a heating mixture stored in a tube running through the center of the can.

THE TIDE TURNS AS THE ALLIES FIGHT BACK

The Allies' strategy is to defeat Italy first and then turn their attention to Germany, and finally Japan. Sicily is first to fall and Italy eventually surrenders. Meanwhile, the arrival of aircraft carriers in the North Atlantic decimates the German submarines that have been preying on the convoy ships, so food and supplies get through once again. The first electromechanical computer grinds into action in the U.K., decoding German messages. In a Swiss laboratory, Albert Hofmann stumbles into LSD. In New York, the young Francis Albert Sinatra croons his way to stardom.

1943

Jan	5	Botanist and chemist George Washington Carver dies at age 82
	18	Siege of Leningrad comes to an end
Apr	18	Uprising by the inhabitants of the Warsaw Ghetto
May	18	The Dambusters raid
July	10	Allies invade Sicily
Sep	8	Axis Powers broken as Italy surrenders
Nov	28	Churchill, Roosevelt, and Stalin meet in Tehran

ABOVE: Increasing numbers of women go to work in factories to replace the men who have gone to war.

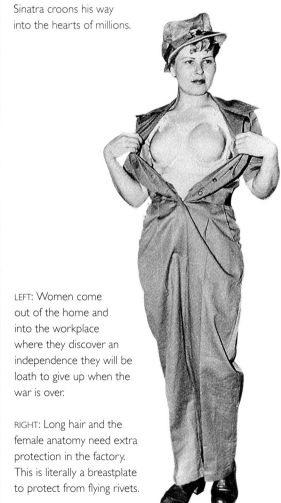

ABOVE: Teen idol Frank Sinatra croons his way into the hearts of millions.

LEFT: Women come out of the home and into the workplace where they discover an independence they will be loath to give up when the war is over.

RIGHT: Long hair and the female anatomy need extra protection in the factory. This is literally a breastplate to protect from flying rivets.

ABOVE: In Katyn Forest, the bodies of 4,000 Polish officers, identifiable only by their army papers, are uncovered.

BELOW: President Roosevelt cuts his birthday cake while returning from the Casablanca Conference.

THE CASABLANCA AGREEMENT

Churchill and Roosevelt meet in Casablanca, Morocco, and agree to fight for the unconditional surrender of Germany, Italy, and Japan. The Allies agree to invade Italy to force it out of the war.

HORROR IN KATYN FOREST

German forces discover the bodies of more than 4,000 Polish Army officers in a mass grave in the Katyn Forest at Smolensk, U.S.S.R.. Germany accuses the U.S.S.R. of their deaths. The murders cause considerable tension between the U.S.S.R. and the Polish government in exile in London.

VICTORY IN THE NORTH ATLANTIC

The campaign by German U-boats against Allied shipping begins to falter as Allied planes flying from aircraft carriers released from the campaign in North Africa are able to hunt down the U-boats at sea. Throughout 1942, more than 650,000 tons of shipping is lost each month, but by May 1943 the figure drops to 18,000 tons in a month, with 17 U-boats sunk. Success in the North Atlantic increases supplies of food and vital war materials to Britain.

SICILY FALLS

The Allies invade Sicily. Mussolini is dismissed by King Victor Emmanuel and the new government surrenders unconditionally in September. As a result, German troops pour into Italy to defend its former ally, while Mussolini proclaims a new Italian republic from the northern town of Salò, on Lake Garda.

SEYFERT GALAXIES

American astronomer Carl K. Seyfert discovers that a small number of galaxies contain unusually bright nuclei and emit radio waves and infrared energy; they are now called Seyfert Galaxies.

THE ACCIDENTAL TRIPPER

LSD (lysurgic acid diethylamide) is accidentally discovered by a Swiss chemist, Albert Hofmann of Sandoz AG, whose description of a "trip" inspires further research.

THE TEHRAN STRATEGY

The three leaders of Russia, United States, and Britain meet together for the first time in the Iranian capital, Tehran, to discuss the war. Churchill and Roosevelt outline their plans to invade France.

BOUNCING BOMBS

Flying Lancaster bombers, the RAF's 617 Squadron, led by Guy Gibson, successfully use specially designed bombs to blow up the Mohne and Eder dams at Mulheim and Dortmund in Germany. The bombs, which bounce along the water like stones skipping on a pond, have been designed by English aeroengineer Barnes Wallis (1887–1979).

STOP THE PRESS

The *Frankfurter Zeitung*, a highly respected newspaper, is suppressed by Hitler. After the war, it is replaced by the *Algemeine Zeitung*, and then by the *Frankfurter Algemeine Zeitung*, which pledges to uphold its predecessor's fairness and objectivity.

BEING AND NOTHINGNESS

Existentialist Jean-Paul Sartre's greatest contribution to philosophy is expressed in this book, which explores the opposition between objective things and human consciousness. It sums up the alienation of the intellectual in the postwar era in such phrases as "Man is condemned to be free."

THE QUEBEC PLAN

British and American leaders meeting in Quebec, Canada, agree to the defeat of Germany before Japan, and plan to invade France in May 1944.

O WHAT A BEAUTIFUL MORNING

Richard Rogers and Oscar Hammerstein bring cheer to a world at war with their musical about life and love among the ranchers and farmers in Oklahoma.

KIDNEY DIALYSIS

Working in secret during German occupation of the Netherlands, physician Willem J. Kolff builds the first artificial kidney machine. It temporarily enables waste products to be eliminated from the bloodstream while damaged kidneys recover.

UNDERSEA ADVENTURE

SCUBA (self-contained underwater breathing apparatus) diving equipment, invented by French naval divers Jacques-Yves Cousteau and Emile Gagnan, is tested successfully. Marketed as the Aqualung, it consists of a steel bottle of compressed air and a control valve to supply air at normal pressure while the diver swims freely.

RACE RELATIONS IN THE UNITED STATES

Gunnar Myrdal, a Swedish sociologist commissioned by the Carnegie Foundation, publishes *The American Dilemma*. It is an exhaustive study of race relations in the United States and their relationship to the democratic process.

ZOOT RIOTS

In Los Angeles and Detroit, black and Hispanic youths dressed in flamboyant long and baggy suits clash with white servicemen. Many are injured and 35 people are killed.

GIANT BRAIN

Colossus, the world's first electromechanical computer, goes into service at Bletchley Park, Buckinghamshire, England, to help decode German messages during World War II.

INVASION, LIBERATION, AND RETALIATION

German war hero Colonel von Stauffenberg fails in his assassination attempt on Hitler. The massive operation of the D-Day landings on the Normandy coast leads to success for the Allies and Paris is liberated in August. In retaliation, Hitler sends V-1 and V-2 rockets to bomb London. Away from the war, the World Bank and the International Monetary Fund are established. Franklin D. Roosevelt is returned for an unprecedented fourth term in office as President of the United States.

1944

Jan	23	Norwegian artist Edvard Munch dies at the age of 80
Mar	4	U.S. airplanes attack Berlin in a daytime raid
June	4	Allies and U.S. troops take Rome
	6	D-Day arrives; the Allies invade Normandy at sunrise
	17	Iceland becomes a republic
	22	President Roosevelt signs The G.I. Bill Of Rights into law
Aug	25	Paris is liberated
Sep	2	Brussels is liberated
	9	London is hit by V-2 rockets
Oct	25	As promised, General Douglas MacArthur returns to the Philippines

LEFT: A radar antenna used by the U.S. Army to detect air invasions by the enemy.

ASSASSINATION FOILED

A plot by senior German officers fails to kill Hitler in his eastern headquarters at Rastenburg. The leader of the plot, Count Claus von Stauffenberg, is shot the same evening, with more than 5,000 people executed for complicity over the next few months.

REVOLT IN WARSAW

Citizens of Warsaw rise in revolt against their German occupiers as the Soviet Red Army approaches the city in August. The Russians, however, do nothing to assist the rising, which collapses with the destruction of the city in October by the German Army. Many Poles are killed or exiled, strengthening Russia's hand in Poland.

GAMES OFF AGAIN

The Olympics are again stopped by World War II.

ABOVE: The Eighth Air Force destroy the Focke Wulf plant in Marienburg in one of the first big air raids.

LIBERTY FOR PARIS

Paris is liberated by the Allies. General De Gaulle enters the city in triumph and brings back the provisional government from its exile in Algiers, North Africa. In November 1945, he is elected president of the provisional government.

WORLD BANK ESTABLISHED

An international monetary and financial conference is held at Bretton Woods, New Hampshire, to establish a world economic order based on fixed exchange rates. The World Bank and the International Monetary Fund are set up to provide funds and loans to help the international economy.

(ALTON) GLENN MILLER
(1904–1944)

The American big-band leader is presumed dead, as he was traveling in a small plane that disappeared crossing the English Channel. He began his musical career in 1924 when he joined the Ben Pollack Band and has been a dance band leader since 1937. He was stationed in Europe where his Glenn Miller Air Force Band entertained the troops.

DAME ETHEL MARY SMYTH
(1858–1944)

The English composer and feminist has died. Somewhat eccentric, she composed "The March for Women," the battle song of the Women's Social and Political Union in 1911, and works such as *The Boatswain's Mate* (1916) and the opera *The Wreckers* (first performed in Germany in 1906). Her autobiographical works are *Female Pipings for Eden* (1933) and *What Happened Next* (1940).

HUNGER WINTER
Cut off behind German lines and starved of food in the harsh winter, many people in the Netherlands die of hunger and cold during the winter months before they are liberated in March 1945.

STREPTOMYCIN
Russian-born U.S. microbiologist Selman Waksman isolates the antibiotic streptomycin, which is used to treat tuberculosis.

ICELANDIC INDEPENDENCE
Iceland's parliament votes to become independent from Denmark. Iceland was occupied by British forces in 1940, when Denmark was invaded, to stop it being occupied by the Germans. Since July 1941, it has been garrisoned by U.S. forces.

PIET MONDRIAN (PIETER CORNELIS MONDRIAAN) (1872–1944)

The Dutch painter and founder of the influential De Stijl group has died. He set up the group in the 1920s, concerned with developing modernism in architecture, painting, and design. Apart from early figurative paintings, his work is determinedly abstract, using grid structures and primary colors. In the past six years he has lived in England and then New York City, and he has had a strong influence on modern art.

DOODLEBUGS OVER LONDON
Germany's secret weapon, the pilotless V-1 missile, is launched against the southeast of Britain. The doodlebug, as it is known, contains 1 ton of high explosives and travels at more than 400 miles per hour. Its high impact causes British authorities to order a second mass exodus of more than one million children and their mothers out of the capital to safety in the countryside.

MAN-MADE FIBER
The first yarn is made from polyester fiber, discovered in 1941 by British chemist John Rex Whinfield and marketed as Terylene in the U.K. and Dacron in the United States. It is resistant to heat and wear, and holds its color well.

MORE BOMBS
Despite continuing air raids on Germany, the German Air Force retaliates in February by launching its heaviest raids on London since May 1941. The following month, U.S. bombers begin daylight raids on Berlin.

PAPER CHROMATOGRAPHY
British biochemists Archer J.P. Porter and Richard Synge develop the process of paper chromatography, in which paper filters are used to separate the components of complex chemical mixtures.

SYNTHESIZED QUININE
A synthezised (laboratory-made) form of quinine is created in the United States in 1944, because supplies of quinine are cut off from Europe and North America by Japanese occupation of the East Indies.

ABOVE: Soldiers of the U.S. Women's Army Corps report for duty in Dutch New Guinea.

ABOVE: The Dutch royal family pose in the garden of their temporary home near Ottawa.

MACARTHUR FULFILLS PROMISE

General Douglas MacArthur returns to the Philippines with a convoy of 225,000 men that destroy two divisions of the Japanese fleet in Leyte Gulf.

MECHANICAL CALCULATOR

U.S. data processing pioneer Howard H. Aiken leads a team to build the Harvard Mark I, the world's first automatic sequence controlled calculator. It is mainly mechanical and measures 50 feet long and weighs 4 tons.

A CHILD OF OUR TIME

English composer Michael Tippett (1905–1998) writes the text to this oratorio (which includes traditional spirituals) as well as the music. The subject concerns the real-life incident in which a German diplomat is killed by a young Polish Jew, in a protest on behalf of the thousands of Polish Jews stuck without money, food, or possessions on the border of Poland and prevented from crossing.

THREE STUDIES FOR FIGURES AT THE BASE OF A CRUCIFIXION

These paintings establish Irish painter Francis Bacon (1909–1992) as a major artist. These three monstrous, freakish figures seem to reflect the suffering of the war and to say that the world had changed as a result. They will cause sensation and consternation when they are put on public show in 1945.

THE ARAB LEAGUE

Seven Arab governments, plus representatives of the Palestinians, set up the Arab League to promote inter-Arab links and minimize conflict between Arab nations. A Council is set up in Cairo, Egypt the following year.

DOUBLE INDEMNITY

Barbara Stanwyck and Fred MacMurray play the conspirators, Edward G Robinson the investigator, in the *Film Noir* thriller *Double Indemnity*, co-written by Raymond Chandler and its director Billy Wilder.

ABOVE: General Eisenhower addresses his crack paratroopers prior to takeoff.

AFTERMATH AND ATOMIC BOMBS

After six years of bitter conflict, World War II finally comes to an end. The Allies liberate the death camps, revealing appalling horrors and evidence of the Holocaust. Two atom bombs are dropped on Japan, ushering in a new and terrifying nuclear age. The United Nations is founded with the aim of preventing future conflicts and maintaining global security. The first electronic computer is built.

1945

Jan	17	Soviet Army takes Warsaw, Poland
	27	Soviet troops liberate Auschwitz death camp
Feb	11	Yalta Conference ends. Roosevelt, Stalin, and Churchill plan for Germany's surrender
	13–14	Allies bomb Dresden, Germany
Mar	7	American troops capture Ludendorf Bridge
	9	Les Enfants du Paradis premieres in Paris
	23	Allied armies cross the Rhine
Apr	1	Battle of Okinawa begins
	12	U.S. President Franklin D. Roosevelt dies of a brain hemorrhage at age 63
	28	Benito Mussolini is shot by partisans
	30	Adolf Hitler commits suicide
May	2	Berlin surrenders to Soviet army
	8	VE (Victory in Europe) Day

June	21	U.S. forces complete the capture of Okinawa with massive casualties
July	15	Potsdam Conference begins
	16	U.S. tests first atomic bomb
Aug	6	Atomic bomb dropped on Hiroshima, Japan, by U.S. plane
	9	U.S. plane drops atomic bomb on Nagasaki, Japan
	17	Indonesia proclaims independence
Sep	2	Japan unconditionally surrenders. World War II is over
	26	United Nations formally comes into being
Oct	11	Fighting breaks out in China between Nationalists and Communists
Nov	20	Trial of Nazi leaders begins in Nuremberg, Germany

ABOVE: The horrors of Germany's "final solution" are slowly revealed as the concentration camps are opened up.

DEATH CAMPS LIBERATED

In January, Soviet troops are the first to liberate a death camp when they enter Auschwitz, in Poland, finding just 7,000 inmates alive. Over the next five months, Allied troops liberate all the death and concentration camps in occupied Europe, revealing thousands of badly malnourished and ill-treated inmates. U.S. troops entering Dachau are so appalled at the state of the 33,000 survivors and the piled-up bodies of the dead that they shoot all 500 SS guards within the hour. The exact number who died in the camps is not known, but is thought to total more than six million. Most are Jews, although gypsies, gays, and others defined by the Nazis as "undesirable" have also been killed.

TOKYO FIRE RAIDS

The first incendiary attack against the Japanese capital devastates the city center and kills 100,000 people.

BELOW: One of the few survivors of Japan's bombing of Shanghai.

YALTA CONFERENCE

The three Allied leaders, U.S. President Roosevelt, Soviet Premier Joseph Stalin, and British Prime Minister Winston Churchill, meet at Yalta in the Crimea to plan Germany's unconditional surrender and its division into four parts after the war. They also agree to the fate of Berlin and Poland and make arrangements for the first U.N. conference, to be held in San Francisco. Stalin also agrees to enter the war against Japan when the war in Europe is finished; in return, the Soviet Union will gain control over the north of Korea.

DRESDEN BOMBED

In order to prevent supplies reaching the Eastern Front against Russia, British and U.S. bombers reduce the industrial city of Dresden to ruins, killing between 30,000 and 60,000 civilians. The bombing causes widespread condemnation in Britain. Some attack it for humanitarian reasons, others because it diverts bombers from attacking vital communications and oil supplies.

ABOVE: Churchill, Roosevelt, and Stalin, allied in the fight against Germany, meet at Yalta to discuss the future.

FIGHTING IN THE PHILIPPINES

The Americans launch a combined sea and air attack on the island of Corregidor to liberate Okinawa, Manila, and the tiny island of Iwo Jima. Casualties on both sides are enormous. The capture of the heavily fortified island of Iwo Jima, in particular, provides the Americans with a jumping-off point for bombing raids against Japan.

DEATH OF WAR LEADERS

Three war leaders die within days of each other: Franklin Roosevelt dies of a cerebral hemorrhage and is succeeded by Vice President Harry Truman (1884–1972). Benito Mussolini is shot by Italian partisans, and Adolf Hitler takes his own life.

ABOVE: After Japan's surrender, Lt. Gen. Torashiro Kawabe boards a plane for a conference in Manila.

UNITED NATIONS FOUNDED

The founding conference of the United Nations (UN) begins in April in San Francisco. In June, 51 member nations sign the United Nations Charter. Like the League of Nations, which it supersedes, the aim of the UN is to maintain international peace and security. An International Court of Justice is set up in The Hague, Netherlands.

BLACK BOY

In his autobiography, *Black Boy*, black American writer Richard Wright (1908–1960) is eloquent about the plight of black people.

VE DAY

War in Europe comes to an end in May with the unconditional surrender of Germany. Throughout the continent, people celebrate Victory in Europe (VE) Day on May 8, even though many of its cities are in ruins and food is in scarce supply.

. . . AND THE COMPUTER BUG

Mathematician Grace Murray Hopper, working on a new computer, finds a moth has stopped a relay working. This is the first actual computer "bug."

DAVID LLOYD GEORGE
(1863–1945)

The British Liberal prime minister, who presided over the coalition government during and immediately after World War I (1916–1922), has died. He was in Parliament until the year of his death. Of Welsh parentage and upbringing, he was a fine and fiery orator. As chancellor of the exchequer from 1908 to 1915, he was responsible for the radical "people's budget" of 1909 and introduced pensions, sick pay, and the social insurance system.

HIROSHIMA AND NAGASAKI

In August, U.S. bombers drop atomic bombs on the Japanese cities of Hiroshima and Nagasaki, so initiating the age of nuclear warfare. The atomic bomb on Hiroshima is nicknamed "Little Boy." Dropped by a B-29 piloted by Col. Paul Tibbets, it destroys 47 square miles and kills 70,000 people. The one dropped on Nagasaki is nicknamed "Fat Man" and it kills 24,000 people.

INDONESIA PROCLAIMS INDEPENDENCE

On the surrender of Japan, which was occupying the archipelago, the Indonesian Nationalist Party proclaims independence from the Netherlands, which refuses to recognize the new government. Fighting soon breaks out between the Nationalist Indonesian People's Army and British forces. A truce is declared in November 1946 and again in January 1948.

JAPAN SURRENDERS

The Soviet Union declares war on Japan and invades Manchuria, occupying northern Korea and the northern islands of Japan. Japan surrenders unconditionally, ending the war in the Pacific.

CHINESE CIVIL WAR

Civil war resumes between the nationalists under Chiang Kai-shek (1887–1975) and the Communists, under Mao Zedong (1893–1976) for control of the former Japanese-run province of Manchuria. The war spreads throughout China the following year.

POTSDAM CONFERENCE

Stalin, Churchill, and Truman meet at Potstdam to organize the occupation of Germany. German land east of the Oder-Neisse rivers is to be under Polish jurisdiction, with Austria under four-power control.

VIETNAM DECLARES REPUBLIC

Nationalist and Communist Vietminh forces under Ho Chi Minh (1890–1969) enter Hanoi and force the emperor to abdicate. The following month they declare Vietnam a republic, which the former colonial ruler, France, refuses to recognize.

WAR CRIMES

The Allied International Military Tribunal opens the trial of former Nazi leaders at Nuremberg in Germany. At its conclusion in September 1946, 12 Nazis are sentenced to death, three to life imprisonment, four receive long sentences, and three are acquitted.

BUCHENWALD PHOTOGRAPHS

American photographer Margaret Bourke-White (1906–1971) shows photographs of the concentration camp at Buchenwald, taken when the camp was liberated by the Allies. For the first time, people see the truth about the Nazi atrocities.

ABOVE: Sir Alexander Fleming, who discovered penicillin, explains some of its properties to a grateful former patient.

ANIMAL SATIRE
English author George Orwell (1903–1950) publishes his novel *Animal Farm*. A satire on revolutions, the novel describes how a new tyranny replaces the old when pigs drive out their human masters from the farm, only to turn into something like humans themselves.

HENRY V
British actor Laurence Olivier's film version of Shakespeare's play, *Henry V*, has a special resonance for its British audience. Portraying an England in the grip of a long war in Europe, it reflects Britain's contemporary position and inspires patriotism.

HUIS-CLOS
French existentialist Jean-Paul Sartre (1905–1980) has written a new play, which will become his most famous. Entitled *Huis-Clos* (In Camera), it shows three people trapped in a room in hell.

ABSTRACT EXPRESSIONISM
American painter Jackson Pollock (1912–1956) is one of the leaders of this rising art movement. His technique of drip painting seems random, but enables him to create works of striking beauty and energy.

LES ENFANTS DU PARADIS
French actor Jean-Louis Barrault (1910–1994) plays the mime Deburau in the film version of Marcel Carné's romantic theatre drama, *Les Enfants du Paradis*. The film becomes an instant classic.

ENTER ENIAC . . .
The first completely electronic computer, ENIAC (Electronic Numerical Integrator And Calculator) is built at the University of Pennsylvania. It weighs more than 27 tons and has 18,000 valves.

FRANKLIN DELANO ROOSEVELT (1882–1945)

The American Democratic president Franklin D. Roosevelt, who has seen the United States almost through to the end of World War II, has died. He had been president since 1932, winning four successive elections. He introduced the New Deal that helped the United States out of the Great Depression, devised the Lend-Lease deal of 1940–1941, whereby the United States supplied arms to Britain, and was instrumental in sorting out postwar Europe at Yalta shortly before his death.

"MISSING" ELEMENT FOUND
Element 61, the rare-earth metal promethium, is found by three U.S. chemists, Charles D. Coryell, Lawrence E. Glendenin and J. A. Marinsky. This discovery fills the last gap in the table of the elements.

SIGNALING THE MOON
American and Hungarian experts simultaneously reflect radar signals from the Moon back to Earth.

FIRST ATOM BOMB TESTED
In July, U.S. scientists led by American nuclear physicist Professor Robert Oppenheimer (1904–1967) test the first atomic bomb in the desert at Alamogordo, New Mexico. It produces a 4,000-foot-high mushroom cloud.

PATTON IS DEAD
General George S. Patton has died from injuries suffered in a car accident in Germany. He will be buried among the soldiers who died in the Battle of the Bulge in Luxembourg.

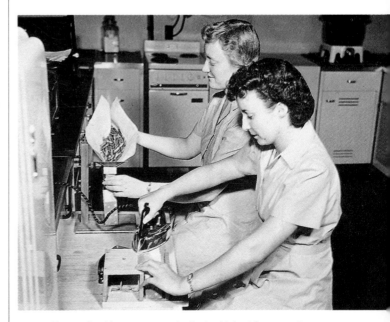

ABOVE: Frozen food becomes popular in the United States and many Americans freeze and pack their own at home.

THE ATOMIC BOMB

ABOVE: The Enola Gay in a dispersal area after its mission against Hiroshima.

ABOVE: The plutonium "Fat Man" bomb is used against Nagasaki.

ABOVE: The Enola Gay's crew receive their final preflight instructions.

RIGHT: The awesome cloud billows above Nagasaki.

INSET: This victim's burns have etched her skin with the pattern of her kimono.

ABOVE AND BELOW: Evidence of the dreadful destructive power of the world's first atomic weapons.

THE IRON CURTAIN COMES DOWN

The United Nations holds its opening session but the first signs of the Cold War appear as former British Prime Minister, Winston Churchill, warns of an "Iron Curtain" dividing Communist countries from non-Communist countries in Europe. The word "bikini" enters the language from an American atomic testing at Bikini Atoll and a new "explosive" swimsuit. Paris becomes a center for bohemian writers and artists, and espresso coffee is the new craze from Italy.

1946

Jan	10	First session of United Nations opens in London	**June**	4	Juan Perón is elected president of Argentina
	20	General de Gaulle resigns as president of France	**July**	4	Philippines becomes independent of U.S. rule
Feb	1	Norwegian Trygve Lie is elected president of the U.N.		5	Bikini swimsuit displayed in Paris
	14	IBM introduces the world's fastest calculator, the ENIAC (Electronic Numerical Integrator and Computer)	**Oct**	3	United Nations General Assembly meets in New York
Mar	5	Churchill delivers his "Iron Curtain" speech in Fulton, Missouri	**Nov**	23	French troops bomb Haiphong, Vietnam, killing around 20,000. The French Indochinese War begins.
	6	France recognizes the Democratic Republic of Vietnam	**Dec**	20	French troops occupy Hanoi, the capital of Vietnam. Ho Chi Minh calls for resistance to the French
May	5	Civil war breaks out in Greece		25	Comedian W.C. Fields dies on Christmas day at the age of 66
June	2	Italy votes for a republic			

OPPOSITE: An atomic, or "mushroom" cloud, rising from Bikini Atoll in the Marshall Islands, the site of nuclear weapon testing by the United States in the 1940s and 1950s.

ABOVE: General Charles De Gaulle resigns as head of France's provisional postwar government after only two months in the post. More than ten years later, he is once again elected president by the people of France, a position he holds for over a decade.

DE GAULLE RESIGNS
In France, General de Gaulle (1890–1970) resigns as French president because of continued Communist opposition to his rule.

PERON ELECTED PRESIDENT
Juan Perón (1895–1974) is elected president of Argentina. He first came to power as one of the leading officers who took over the government in 1943 and consolidated his power among both the army and the workers. In October 1945, he briefly lost power in a U.S. sponsored coup, but was quickly returned to power. Much of his popularity is due to his wife, Eva.

GREEK WAR
Civil war breaks out in Greece between the monarchist Democratic Army of Greece (DSE) backed by Britain, and the Communist National Popular Liberation Army (ELAS) backed by Albania, Bulgaria, and Yugoslavia. In September, a plebiscite agrees to restore the monarchy. Fighting continues until the defeat of the Communists in October 1949.

IRON CURTAIN
Making a speech in Fulton, Missouri, British wartime leader Winston Churchill (1874–1964) warns that an "Iron Curtain" is descending in Europe from the Baltic to the Adriatic, as the U.S.S.R. strengthens its grip on Eastern Europe. For many people, this speech marks the beginning of what becomes known as the Cold War.

FRENCH INDOCHINESE WAR
France recognizes the creation of the Democratic Republic of Vietnam, headed by the Communist leader Ho Chi Minh, as part of a French-led Indochinese Federation. Relations between France and Ho Chi Minh break down and in November, the French bomb the northern port of Haiphong, killing around 20,000 people, as they seek to maintain control of Vietnam. This marks the start of a war which lasts until 1954.

ZORBA THE GREEK
The novel *Zorba the Greek* by Nikos Kazantzakis (1883–1957) is published. His portrayal of Zorba and his passionate love of life is a success in Greece and will soon be widely translated.

ITALIAN REPUBLIC
A referendum in Italy produces a huge majority for a republic. King Umberto II (1904–1983) goes into exile; the prime minister, Alcide de Gasperi (1881–1954), becomes provisional head of state. The Allies agree to transfer the Italian-owned Dodecanese Islands to Greece, some lands to Yugoslavia, and parts of northern Italy to France.

ITALIAN WOMEN GAIN THE VOTE
In June, Italian women gain the right to vote in national elections for the first time.

RIOTS IN INDIA
More than 3,000 people die as Muslims and Hindus clash in Calcutta, India. The riots are the culmination of unrest caused by British proposals for Indian independence.

PHILIPPINES INDEPENDENT
In July, the Philippines become independent of U.S. rule.

THE HOUSE OF BERNARDO ALBA
This year sees the publication of *The House of Bernardo Alba*, the last tragedy to have been written by Spanish poet Federico Garcia Lorca (1899–1936). Performed in 1945, nine years after the writer's death, it confirms his stature as Spain's greatest modern dramatist.

ATOMIC TESTING
Americans explode the first of several atomic bombs over Bikini Atoll in the Marshall Islands of the Pacific Ocean. The purpose is to test the bomb's affects on warships and animals.

JOHN MAYNARD KEYNES
(1883–1946)

The English economist and patron of the arts John Maynard Keynes has died. He was a Treasury advisor during both World War I and World War II and put forward the theory of the planned economy. He greatly influenced Franklin D. Roosevelt's New Deal and helped set up the International Monetary Fund. His two major works, *A Treatise on Money* (1930) and *General Theory of Employment, Interest and Money* (1936), were written in response to the unemployment crisis.

ABOVE: Renowned American art collector and politician Nelson A. Rockefeller. He goes on to become the 41st vice president of the United States.

ESPRESSO COFFEE

The Gaggia coffee machine is invented in Italy; it uses steam to produce espresso coffee, which rapidly becomes popular.

EXPLOSIVE BIKINI

French fashion designer Louis Réard displays an abbreviated two-piece bathing costume for women in Paris; he calls it a "bikini" because he thinks its effect is as explosive as the bomb just tested.

PATERSON

American poet William Carlos Williams begins to publish his long poem, *Paterson*; he will add to it for the rest of his life. Using a collage of anecdotes, letters, reports, conversations, and more traditional "poetic" passages, the poem attempts to create a typically American work of art by describing the everyday life of ordinary Americans.

EJECTOR SEAT

British aeronautical engineer James Martin, using dummies, makes the first tests of an ejector seat to enable pilots to escape from crashing aircraft.

MEMOIRS OF HECATE COUNTRY

American writer and critic Edmund Wilson (1895–1972) publishes this collection of short stories. It is accused of obscenity and banned in some jurisdictions, so becoming a bestseller in others.

ZOOM LENS

U.S. scientist Frank Back of the Zoomar Corporation develops the first zoom lens for cameras.

BOHEMIAN QUARTIER

The Paris quarter of St. Germain-des-Prés becomes the focus of writers, artists, and musicians, including the existentialist Jean-Paul Sartre, feminist Simone de Beauvoir, and sculptor Alberto Giacometti.

BELOW: East meets West as Allies (pictured in 1945). This year, rifts emerge and the alliance shows signs of disintegration.

NEW COUNTRIES AND A BABY BOOM

India is partitioned into two separate, independent countries: India and Pakistan. The partition causes conflict. The U.N. votes to divide Palestine, a decision that also leads to conflict. The Marshall Plan is introduced to rebuild Europe. A U.S. pilot is the first to break the sound barrier, women's fashion adopts a "New Look" and Method acting takes to the stage. This year also sees the start of the "baby boom" and a liberal approach to child rearing.

1947

Jan	21	General George Marshall becomes the Secretary of State
	23	French painter Pierre Bonnard dies at the age of 80
	25	Chicago gangster Al "Scarface" Capone dies
Feb	12	French designer Christian Dior launches the "New Look"
Mar	12	U.S. President Truman outlines "Truman Doctrine"
	19	Chinese Nationalists capture Communist capital, Yan'an
	25	John D. Rockefeller, Jr. donates land in New York City for the construction of the United Nations
Apr	7	Automobile manufacturer Henry Ford dies at the age of 83
	15	Jackie Robinson is first black American in major league baseball
June	5	U.S. Secretary of State George Marshall calls for aid for Europe
	15	Anne Frank's diary is published
July	5	American Jack Kramer wins the mens championship at Wimbledon
Aug	15	India and Pakistan are granted their independence from Britain
	31	The U.N. proposes to partition Palestine into two states
Oct	14	U.S. pilot Chuck Yeager breaks the sound barrier
Nov	2	Howard Hughes' "Spruce Goose" takes to the air
	29	United Nations announces plan for the partition of Palestine
Dec	4	Tennessee Williams' play "A Streetcar Named Desire" opens

LEFT AND BELOW: Reclusive millionaire businessman Howard Hughes in the cockpit of his 400,000-pound "Spruce Goose," the world's largest plane, at Long Beach, California. A record-breaking pilot, Hughes is set to take the eight-engined aircraft to speeds of 100 miles per hour .

TRUMAN DOCTRINE
In response to Britain's announcement that it can no longer afford to keep troops in Greece to fight the Communists in the civil war, President Truman plans to give aid to both the Greek and Turkish governments to protect them from Communism. This becomes the Truman Doctrine, under which the United States offers to support "free peoples who are resisting attempted subjugation by armed minorities or by outside pressures."

MARSHALL PLAN
U.S. Secretary of State George Marshall (1880–1959) announces massive financial aid for European nations to enable them to rebuild their economies after the war. The Marshall Plan, as it is known, is accepted in Western Europe but rejected by those Eastern European nations occupied by the U.S.S.R.

CARBON-14 DATING
U.S. chemist Willard F. Libby (1908–1980) and co-workers perfect carbon-14 dating, by which the amount of this decaying radioactive material left in organic remains shows how long they have been dead.

INDIA PARTITIONED
Britain partitions the Indian Empire, granting India and Pakistan independence, with Burma and Ceylon to follow the next year. Partition brings to an end more than 160 years of British rule. Fighting breaks out between India and Pakistan over the state of Kashmir, whose Muslim population riots in favor of joining, but whose Hindu leader wishes to join India. Many millions die across the subcontinent in inter-communal fighting.

THE NEW LOOK
French fashion designer Christian Dior launches a sensational "New Look." After the austerity of the war years, Dior's look, with its generous use of material, nipped-in waist, soft shoulders and billowing skirts, is welcomed by women with enthusiasm.

FIGHTING IN PALESTINE
Britain hands back the mandate for Palestine to the U.N. because it is unable to control the country. The U.N. votes to partition Palestine with separate homelands for Jews and Palestinians. Both sides disagree and fighting soon breaks out.

ABOVE: Record snowfalls hit New York City in December 1947, making it necessary to shift as much of the snow as possible into the East River at Manhattan.

BELOW: American pilot Captain Charles "Chuck" Yeager becomes the first person to break the sound barrier, in his rocket-propelled Bell X-1 aircraft.

ACTOR'S STUDIO

Founded by Elia Kazan, Robert Lewis, and Cheryl Crawford, the Actor's Studio in New York City propounds and popularizes the Stanislavski Method in the United States. Many well-known American actors will be trained here, especially during the 1950s.

HIGHER EDUCATION BOOMS

Colleges and universities everywhere are swamped by applications for admission. In the United States, where many colleges closed down or were almost bankrupted during the war, applications reach an all-time high of more than two million thanks to the G.I. Bill.

UFOs

Unidentified Flying Objects (UFOs) are reported in Washington State, first by a pilot, Kenneth Arnold, and later by members of the public. The many reports of flying saucer-shaped objects illuminating the night sky are ridiculed by the United States Air Force.

BRANDO STARS IN STREETCAR

Tennessee Williams' play, *A Streetcar Named Desire*, opens with Marlon Brando (1924 – 2004) in the role of Stanley Kowalski. Brando uses the Stanislavski Method of acting, which emphasizes realism and an understanding of the psychology of the character, rather than a declamatory approach.

ABOVE: American Method actor Marlon Brando makes his stage breakthrough in the Tennessee Williams play *A Streetcar Named Desire*. Brando goes on to star in the film version of the play and to become one of the most famous screen actors in the world.

ABOVE: The great baseball player Jackie Robinson becomes the first black player to play outside the Negro Leagues when he joins the Brooklyn Dodgers. Robinson's outstanding performances are a major step in overcoming racial bigotry in sport in the United States.

THE "HOLLYWOOD TEN"

Ten American directors and screenwriters refuse to testify before the House Un-American Activities Committee, which is obsessed with hunting out alleged Communists. The "ten" are given one year jail sentences, signalling the beginning of "witch hunting" in the cinema world and elsewhere.

ANNE FRANK'S DIARY

The diary of a young Jewish girl, Anne Frank, who died in 1945 in a concentration camp, is published, providing a remarkable insight into the Holocaust. The story of her family's concealment from, and eventual discovery by, the Nazis in Amsterdam becomes known all over the world.

BENELUX FORMED

A customs union is formed by Belgium, the Netherlands and Luxembourg. It is known as the Benelux customs union, an acronym of Belgium, Netherlands, and Luxembourg.

SUPERSONIC FLIGHT

In October, Charles "Chuck" Yeager, a U.S. Army pilot, becomes the first man to fly faster than the speed of sound (1,125 feet per second), flying a Bell X1 rocket plane.

CHLORAMPHENICOL DISCOVERED

Scientists discover chloramphenicol, a broad-spectrum antibiotic. In some patients, it causes damage to the bone marrow, so its use is confined to severe infections that safer drugs cannot touch.

STRONG FORCE FOUND

British chemist Cecil F. Powell discovers the pion, a subatomic particle that produces a "strong force" that holds an atom's nucleus together.

ALPHONSE (AL) CAPONE (1899–1947)

American gangster Al Capone, sometimes known as Scarface, has died. He joined a street gang as a boy and during the prohibition era amassed a fortune and notoriety. The infamous St. Valentine's Day Massacre of 1929 was fought between his and a rival gang. Sent to jail in 1931 on tax fraud charges, Capone was released early on health grounds and spent the remainder of his life on his Florida estate.

CRAB NEBULA

Australian radio astronomers discover that the Crab Nebula is a strong radio source. The nebula is the gaseous remains of a supernova, a star which exploded in 1054.

TRANSISTOR INVENTED

U.S. physicists John Bardeen, Walter Brattain, and William Schockley invent the transistor, a tiny electronic device that controls electric current; it revolutionizes all electronic apparatus.

POLAROID CAMERA

U.S. scientist Edwin H. Land (1909–1991) invents and demonstrates the Polaroid Land Camera™, which can produce a print seconds after a picture is taken.

HELL'S ANGELS ARRIVE

The Hell's Angels, a Harley-Davidson biker gang, cause a riot when they converge on the town of Hollister, California. Dressed in leather, bikers in the thousands roam California breaking the law in a quest for thrills.

BABY BOOM

A baby boom begins, with 3,411,000 births recorded in the United States. In the U.K., there are 20.5 births per 1000, 20% more than the 1939 figure.

MICROWAVE OVENS

The first microwave ovens are sold in the United States. Invented in 1945 by Percy LeBaron Spencer after a factory radar power tube melted a chocolate bar in his pocket, they are bulky and designed for use in commercial food preparation.

JACKIE ROBINSON

Jackie Robinson becomes the first African-American to play baseball in the major leagues. He plays for the Brooklyn Dodgers and paves the way for racial integration of the American pastime.

DEAD SEA SCROLLS

The Dead Sea Scrolls are discovered when a Bedouin boy, Muhammad ad-Dibh, explores a cave at Qumran in Jordan and finds an earthenware jar containing leather and parchment scrolls. They were written by the Essenes, a Jewish sect of the 1st century B.C.

PERSONALITY DIMENSIONS

Hans Eysenck (1916–1997), a British psychologist, publishes *Dimensions of Personality*, a study of neuroticism and extrovert behavior. He argues that personality is biologically determined and criticizes psychoanalysis because it does not increase the likelihood of recovery from the disorder being treated.

LIBERAL CHILD CARE

American pediatrician Benjamin Spock (1903–1998) publishes *The Common Sense Book of Baby and Child Care*. It is the first practical manual of childcare, which he wrote while serving in the army. He rejects authoritative child-raising methods and advocates a liberal upbringing.

DOMESTIC ELECTRIC BLENDER

An electric blender is produced for home use in the United States. Invented in 1919, it was used only in commercial kitchens until Frederick J. Ossius introduces the Waring Blender, named after band leader Fred Waring.

HENRY FORD
(1863–1947)

American car manufacturer Henry Ford, who founded the Ford Motor Company in 1903, has died. He introduced the assembly line technique, which allowed cars to be produced with great efficiency "on the line." While refusing to accept unionization, he paid unusually high wages, even when this was in opposition to government policy under the New Deal. He set up the Ford Foundation. Always eccentric, at the age of 82 shortly before his death, he attempted to regain control of the Ford Motor Company from his grandson.

OPPOSITE ABOVE: U.S. Secretary of State George Catlett Marshall puts forward the European Recovery Program, better known as the Marshall Plan, which helps to put postwar Europe back on its feet. About $13 million is spent on aid for Europe in the form of food and machinery. Here a U.S. cargo ship fills its hold with supplies.

ABOVE: Not only Europe benefits from the Marshall Plan. Flour and rice are shipped to North Africa, which was also a battleground in World War II.

RIGHT: Equipment, vehicles, and machinery are also part of the plan. Although the driving motive is to contain the spread of Communism in Europe, the Marshall Plan certainly helps nations to recover as quickly as possible from the devastation of war.

BERLIN BLOCKADE AND A NEW ISRAEL

Indian leader Gandhi is assassinated and in South Africa, the incoming Nationalist government introduces apartheid, a policy of racial separation. The independent state of Israel comes into being, leading to an immediate Arab-Israeli conflict. Communist forces in China move to capture Beijing and the Berlin Airlift breaks the Soviet blockade of West Germany. The Olympic Games return to the sporting calendar and American sexologist, Alfred Kinsey, exposes the reality of male sexual behavior.

1948

Jan	30	Mahatma Gandhi is assassinated by extremist Hindu, Nathuram Godse
	30	Winter Games begin in St. Moritz
Feb	11	Soviet film director Sergei Eisenstein dies
	18	Irish Prime Minister Eamon de Valera resigns
	20	Communists seize power in Czechoslovakia
May	14	Independent State of Israel is proclaimed
	15	Egypt, Jordan, Syria, Iraq, and Lebanon invade Israel
	28	Jan Smuts ousted in election, South Africa
June	16	Malayan Communists begin campaign against British
	24	Berlin Airlift begins
June	28	Yugoslavia is expelled from the Cominform
July	5	National Health Service is introduced in Britain
	29	Olympic Games open in London
Aug	16	U.S. baseball star "Babe" Ruth dies
Sep	4	Queen Wilhelmina of Holland abdicates after 50 years on the throne
	9	North Korea declares independence as the People's Republic of Korea led by Kim Il Sun
Dec	10	U.N. Assembly adopts Declaration of Human Rights
	10	T.S. Eliot wins the Nobel Prize for literature
	15	Dutch troops seize Jakarta, Indonesia

ABOVE: Czech figure skating champion Aja Vrzanova practicing her art before the 1948 Winter Olympics in St. Moritz. World War II led to the cancellation of the 1940 and 1944 Games.

INDEPENDENT ISRAEL

On the day the British mandate ends, the Jewish National Council and the General Zionist Council proclaim an independent State of Israel, with David Ben-Gurion (1886–1973) as prime minister and Chaim Weizmann (1874–1952) as president. Both the United States and Soviet Union recognize the new state.

ARAB-ISRAELI WAR

Five Arab armies from Egypt, Jordan, Syria, Iraq, and Lebanon attack Israel on the day after its independence. The Israelis hold the attacks and then counterattack. Fighting continues until cease-fires are declared in 1949. Borders are stabilized with Jerusalem divided, but accessible by a narrow corridor of land. The Israelis suffer 8,000 casualties and the Arabs about 20,000.

HALE TELESCOPE

The Hale telescope, with a 16 foot glass mirror, the largest of its time, is officially dedicated at Mt. Palomar, California. It was designed by astrophysicist George E. Hale (1868–1938).

THE NAKED AND THE DEAD

U.S. journalist Norman Mailer (b. 1923) publishes his first novel, *The Naked and the Dead*, marking his emergence as a writer. A realistic novel based on his army experiences in the Pacific, it is considered one of the best American books about World War II.

OAS

The Organization of American States (OAS) is formed to link together all the countries in the Americas.

NATIONALISTS TAKE POWER

In South Africa, Jan Smuts is defeated in the general election by the extreme right wing Afrikaaner Nationalist Party. Douglas Malan (1874–1959) becomes prime minister and introduces legislation for the apartheid system of racial separation, to ensure white supremacy in South Africa.

MALAYAN EMERGENCY

In June, the Malayan Races Liberation Army (MRLA), largely ethnic Chinese Communists, begins a violent campaign against the British government. The MRLA campaign includes sabotage, assassination, and terrorism. The British respond with a variety of tactics including resettling populations and long-range patrols. The MLRA are defeated in 1957, although emergency regulations remain in place until 1960.

CRY, THE BELOVED COUNTRY

South African writer Alan Paton (1903–88) publishes this novel describing the experiences of Rev. Stephen Kumalo, who leaves his township for Johannesburg, where he discovers that tragedies have overtaken the lives of his sister and son. The book eloquently puts the case for understanding between the races.

CAMERA IN LONDON

Photographs by Bill Brandt (1904–1983) show a peaceful London, in acknowledgement of the war's ending. He evokes a city lit by soft sunlight or the light of the moon. They are in contrast to Brandt's earlier, starker wartime series, such as *A Night in London*.

COMMUNIST COUP

The Communist Party stages a coup in Czechoslovakia and takes over the government. The following month, in March, the popular foreign secretary, Jan Masaryk, is found dead outside his flat; many suspect the Communists of murdering him. Throughout the year, Communist governments strengthen their hold on power throughout Eastern Europe.

ABOVE: An American skier takes part in the women's downhill event in the Fifth Winter Olympics.

ABOVE: A replica of the Brandenburg Gate is set up in Berlin to demonstrate against its postwar placement in the Soviet-occupied sector of the city. The slogan reads "Freedom Will Win" and the bear portrayed on the flags is the emblem of Berlin.

YUGOSLAVIA EXPELLED
The U.S.S.R. expels Yugoslavia from Cominform, the Communist Information Bureau designed to coordinate Communist Party activities throughout Europe, because of policy differences with Joseph Stalin. Over the next decade Yugoslav leader Tito, the name adopted by Joseph Broz (1892–1980), gains increasing support from Western Europe in his confrontation with the U.S.S.R.

TURANGALILA SYMPHONY
This huge ten movement symphony, for large orchestra plus piano and ondes Martenot, is described by its French composer Olivier Messiaen (1908–1992) as a love song or a hymn to joy. Its exotic sound world makes it the composer's most popular work.

QUEEN WILHELMINA ABDICATES
In the Netherlands, Queen Wilhelmina abdicates due to ill health. She has been queen for 50 years. She is succeeded by her daughter Juliana (1909–2004).

HUMAN RIGHTS
The United Nations adopts the Universal Declaration of Human Rights, recognizing the rights and freedom from oppression and slavery of all humans, regardless of race, sex, social status, language, religion, and color. Much of the work in drafting the charter is done by Eleanor Roosevelt (1884–1962), widow of the former U.S. president and a delegate to the U.N.

CHINESE CIVIL WAR
In China, the Communists have gained the upper hand, defeating the Nationalists and taking Manchuria. The Nationalists under Chiang Kai-shek retreat southwards. The Communists take Peking and declare a Communist state in northern China. By November, the Nationalists have retreated behind the Great Wall.

INDONESIA
Hostilities continue in Indonesia. Dutch airborne forces seize Jakarta, capturing Ahmed Sukarno's government.

THE PISAN CANTOS
U.S. poet Ezra Pound (1885–1972) publishes *The Pisan Cantos*, an installment of his epic poem, *The Cantos*. It was conceived while Pound was in an American prison camp during World War II, for alleged treacherous broadcasts, and completed when he was detained in a mental hospital.

CHRISTINA'S WORLD
U.S. artist Andrew Wyeth paints his paralyzed neighbor, Anna Christina Olson, against a background of an open horizon and a house. The painting, which becomes one of the artist's best known, shows Wyeth's ability to suggest the limited world of the disabled woman, as well as reflecting his love of the scenery around his Maine summer home.

NATIONAL HEALTH
In Britain, the National Health Service is formed. It is one of the first comprehensive health services in the world. The service provides free healthcare to all, "from the cradle to the grave."

LONG-PLAYING RECORDS
By using plastics instead of shellac, American record companies are able to introduce long-playing records, at two speeds, 33.5 rpm and 45 rpm.

MARTIAN ATMOSPHERE
Dutch-born U.S. astronomer Gerard P. Kuiper (1905–1973) predicts that the atmosphere of Mars is mostly carbon dioxide, a fact later proved by space probes. He also discovers Miranda, the fifth moon of the planet Uranus.

FIRST ATOMIC CLOCK
The first atomic clock is built at the U.S. National Bureau of Standards, in Washington, D.C. It is accurate to one second in 300 years. Later, atomic clocks are accurate to one second in 200,000 years.

BATHYSCAPHE INVENTED
Swiss physicist Auguste Piccard (1884–1962) invents the bathyscaphe, a deep-sea diving craft, and tests it at a depth of 4,495 feet. It now makes deep ocean exploration possible.

NUCLEAR STRUCTURE
Physicists Hans Jensen of Germany and German-born Maria Goeppert Mayer of the United States independently discover the structure of atomic nuclei.

TUBELESS TIRES
The American Goodyear Company introduces the tubeless tire for motor vehicles.

MAHATMA ("GREAT SOUL") GANDHI (1869–1948)

Indian leader Mahatma Gandhi has been assassinated. Venerated as a great pacifist leader, patriot, and social reformer, Gandhi trained as a lawyer. He gave up a lucrative practice to live in South Africa, where he spent 20 years opposing discrimination. In 1914, he returned to India and, although an ardent supporter of Britain, spearheaded the campaign for Indian independence. He was committed to nonviolent civil disobedience but his various campaigns, including the salt march of the 1930s, brought him several terms of imprisonment.

In 1946, he negotiated independence with the British Cabinet Mission. His last months were clouded by Muslim-Hindu strife.

DELVING INTO THE ATOM

U.S. physicist Richard Feynman (1918–1988) develops the theory of quantum electrodynamics, the interaction between the subatomic particles, electrons, photons, and positrons.

CYBERNETICS INVENTED

U.S. statistician Norbert Wiener invents and names a new branch of science: cybernetics, the study of information control in animals and machines.

RECREATING EARLY NAVIGATION

Thor Heyerdahl (b. 1914), a Norwegian ethnographer, sails from Peru with a Scandinavian crew on a balsa wood raft built using techniques known to the Incas. After sailing and drifting more than 5,000 miles, he has reached the Tuamotu archipelago, proving that Pre-Columbian people could have crossed the Pacific and colonized Polynesia.

FIRST SNEAKERS

Adidas of Germany, a sportswear manufacturer, develops sneakers from war surplus canvas and fuel tank rubber. Their first shoe, designed by Adolf Dassler, is decorated with three white stripes.

VELCRO DEVELOPED

Velcro fastening is invented by a Swiss engineer, George de Mestral, inspired by spiny burrs found sticking to his clothing and his dog's coat after a walk.

DEWEY DEFEATS TRUMAN???

In one of the biggest upsets in presidential election history, President Truman defeats Republican favorite Thomas E. Dewey. The *Chicago Daily Tribune* mistakenly prints the infamous morning headline of "Dewey Defeats Truman."

PLANNED PARENTHOOD

The International Planned Parenthood Federation is founded by American social reformer and founder of the birth control movement, Margaret Sanger.

ABORTION ON DEMAND

As the population of Japan approaches 80 million, and in response to increased fetal abnormalities resulting from the 1945 nuclear explosions, the Eugenic Protection Law authorizes abortion on demand.

WINTER GAMES

The Fifth Winter Games are held in St. Moritz, Switzerland, where the facilities have survived World War II unscathed. However, postwar shortages mean hardship for athletes and few visitors. Downhill races for men and women are added to the events, indicating the growing importance of alpine events.

SUMMER OLYMPICS

The Olympic games are held in London, England, which was the proposed site for the cancelled 1944 games. Events are beset by scarcity and competitors live in army barracks, but crowds flock to Wembley for the games. Athlete Fanny Blankers-Koen, a mother of two, and nicknamed the "flying housewife," takes four gold medals back to Holland.

SKYDIVING

Frenchman Leo Valentin develops the modern sport of skydiving by discovering that arching the back is the way to control free fall before opening the parachute.

ABOVE : American Flying Wing aircraft, notable for the absence of tails and fuselages, which shortens their overall length to about a third of other planes. These super efficient new bombers are pictured at Hawthorne, California.

GEORGE HERMAN (BABE) RUTH (1895–1948)

The American baseball player and coach "Babe" Ruth has died. He played in ten World Series and has set a record for home runs that will not be broken until 1974. During his career, he played for the Boston Red Sox (1914–1919), the New York Yankees (1920–1934), and the Boston Braves (1935).

MAKING MOVIES

ABOVE LEFT: The British-born director and producer Alfred Hitchcock (center) is one of early Hollywood's most important figures.

ABOVE RIGHT: Backstage in Hollywood; the romance of a film is created by unsung craftsmen.

RIGHT: The splendor of Hollywood, illuminated by searchlights as a new film is premiered.

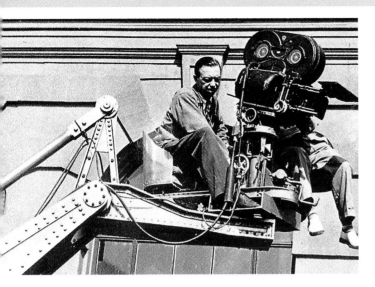

ABOVE: The director surveys the scene from the platform of a movable crane. The use of the crane increases the number of angles from which a shot can be taken on a film set, and improves the overall fluidity of movement.

ABOVE: On location for the film version of Ernest Hemingway's novel *For Whom the Bell Tolls*. The director explains to Ingrid Bergman and Gary Cooper exactly what he has in mind.

RIGHT: The Austrian-born director Fritz Lang (center) is seen explaining a scene of the film *Woman in the Window* to actress Joan Bennett (left). Lang is one of the many European film directors who went to Hollywood when the Nazis came to power.

BELOW: The western is the film genre that distinguishes American movies from those of other cultures. Irish-American John Ford is the maker of many seminal westerns, including *Stagecoach*.

NATO AND THE PEOPLE'S REPUBLIC

Chinese Communists defeat the Kuomintang and set up the People's Republic of China, headed by Mao Zedong. NATO is formed to provide mutual support for western nations and the division of the world into Communist and non-Communist blocs is emphasized by the separation of Germany into East and West. Architecture features glass and steel, a Soviet-U.S. arms race begins, and the novel *1984* warns of a bleak future.

1949

Jan	1	Cease-fire ends India-Pakistan war over Kashmir
	10	Communists capture Xuzhou, China
Apr	4	North Atlantic Treaty Organization (NATO) is formed
	10	Sam Snead wins the Masters Championship in Augusta, Georgia
	16	Western Allies fly 1,398 sorties in 24 hours, delivering 12,937 tons of supplies to Berlin in the greatest number of sorties during the Berlin Airlift
	24	Communist forces advance on Shanghai, China
May	12	Berlin blockade ends
	23	Federal Republic of Germany (West Germany) comes into being
	26	Shanghai falls to Communists, China

July	1	Chemist Linus Pauling discovers the cause of sickle cell anemia
	20	Cease-fire is declared in Arab-Israeli war
Sep	23	Soviet Union tests atomic bomb
	30	Berlin Airlift ends
Oct	1	Mao Zedong proclaims establishment of People's Republic of China
	12	Communist Democratic Republic is established in East Germany
	16	Greek Civil War ends, with defeat of the rebels
Dec	8	Kuomintang (Chinese Nationalists) leave mainland China for Formosa (later Taiwan)
	27	Netherlands transfers sovereignty of Indonesia

ABOVE: Delegates for the United States and the Netherlands add their signatures to the North Atlantic Treaty. The original 12 members include the Netherlands, Britain, France, and the U. S.

NATO AND COUNCIL OF EUROPE

Ten European nations, including the Netherlands and Britain, join with the United States and Canada to form the North Atlantic Treaty Organization (NATO), providing mutual support for each other against aggression. In May, ten Western European nations, including the formerly neutral nations of Sweden and Ireland, set up the Council of Europe to support freedom and the rule of law. The Council meets in Strasbourg and includes a European Court of Human Rights.

WEST AND EAST GERMANY

The United States, Britain, and France merge their three zones in West Germany to create the Federal Republic, which comes into being in May with its capital in Bonn. In September, the Christian Democrat, Konrad Adenauer (1876–1967), becomes chancellor. The following month, the Soviet Union establishes the German Democratic Republic in East Germany.

PEOPLE'S REPUBLIC OF CHINA

Following their victory in the civil war, the Chinese Communist Party establishes the People's Republic under the leadership of Mao Zedong (1893–1976). The Kuomintang Nationalists retreat to the offshore island of Taiwan under the leadership of Chang Kai-shek.

INDONESIA

After lengthy and complex UN-sponsored peace talks, the Netherlands transfers sovereignty to Indonesia under the leadership of President Sukarno (1920-70). Indonesia therefore becomes independent of its former colonial masters, the Dutch. The costs of four years of war include some 25,000 Dutch and 75,000 Indonesian casualties.

ARMS RACE BEGINS

The Soviet Union carries out its first atom bomb test, exploding it at a site in Kazakhstan. This marks the start of an arms race with the United States.

THE THIRD MAN

U.S. actor and director Orson Welles (1915–1985) gives a brilliant performance as Harry Lime in Carol Reed's film *The Third Man*, with a screenplay by Graham Greene. The "Harry Lime Theme" by Anton Karas becomes almost as famous as the film itself.

DEATH OF A SALESMAN

One of the most successful American plays of all time, *Death of a Salesman*, establishes Arthur Miller as a leading American dramatist. It tells the story of the salesman, Willy Loman, who disintegrates because he relies too heavily on the hollow values of modern society.

1984

English author George Orwell's seminal dystopia, *1984*, is published and immediately engages the interest of readers in the English-speaking world and beyond. Many phrases from the book, such as "doublethink" and "Big Brother" find a permanent place in the language.

THE SECOND SEX

French feminist Simone de Beauvoir (1908–86) publishes *The Second Sex*. It draws on art, literature, and philosophy to describe how men have consistently denied the right of humanity to women, and calls for the abolition of the myth of "the eternal feminine." A significant and groundbreaking work, it will later become a key text of the Women's Liberation Movement and a global bestseller.

ABOVE: Chiang Kai-shek moves Nationalist Chinese government to Taiwan.

ABOVE: The new transatlantic flights mean sleeping during the trip. Beds are made up for the passengers of this Constellation aircraft.

ABOVE: Front view of a mechanical calculator that is able to add numbers running into their billions in less than one-fifth of a second.

CONVENIENT CAKES

Cake mixes prepared by General Mills and Pillsbury in the United States increase the range of convenience foods available in the United States.

GLASS HOUSE

Philip Johnson's Glass House in New Canaan, Connecticut, essentially consists of a glass box with a steel frame and is typical of a number of modernist houses currently being designed. Influenced strongly by architect Mies van der Rohe, this house is the perfect example of the tenet "less is more."

NEPTUNE'S MOON

Dutch-born U.S. astronomer Gerard P. Kuiper (1905–1973) discovers the second moon of the planet Neptune, now named Nereid.

ROCKET RECORD

Americans launch the WAC Corporal, a research rocket which reaches the record height of 250 miles; it is launched as a second stage from a V-2 rocket.

MORE ELEMENTS FOUND

American chemists headed by Glenn T. Seaborg create and discover two more elements: numbers 97, berkelium, and 98, californium. They are radioactive rare earths.

SICKLE CELL DISEASE

American biological chemist Linus C. Pauling (1901–1994) discovers that the inherited sickle cell disease is caused by differences in the blood. People with this trait are also found to have immunity from malaria.

INDO-PAKISTAN WAR

Fighting between India and Pakistan ends and Indian troops control Kashmir.

ABOVE: The world's oldest airline, KLM, introduces the "Flying Dutchman," which flies between New York and Amsterdam.

ABOVE: After the war, even neutral Switzerland finds the going tough. The U.S. supplies aid in the form of food.

BERLIN AIRLIFT

Western Allies begin running an airlift to carry supplies into Berlin. Land access to the western sector of Berlin, which is administered by France, Berlin, and the United States, has been blocked off by the Soviet Union. The airlift continues until May 1949, when the Soviet Union relaxes its grip on the city, allowing convoys to use the autobahns across East Germany. A total of 277,264 flights are made, lifting 2,343,315 tons of cargo.

ABOVE: A West German policeman shouts instructions to waiting crowds of East Germans in Berlin as food parcels are distributed in the second joint American-West German food relief program.

ABOVE: Mini-parachutes drop sweets and chewing gum for German children.

LEFT: The baby's carriage seems an ideal place to hide cans of food received as part of the joint American-West German food relief program.

BELOW: C-54 Skymasters unload their cargoes at Templehof Air Force Base.

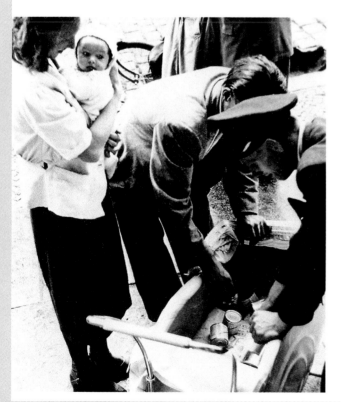

WINNERS AND ACHIEVERS OF THE 1940s

ACADEMY AWARDS

The Academy of Motion Picture Arts and Sciences was founded in 1927 by the movie industry to honor its artists and craftsmen. All categories of motion picture endeavor are honored, but the most significant are listed below.

BEST ACTOR

1940 James Stewart *The Philadelphia Story*
1941 Gary Cooper *Sergeant York*
1942 James Cagney *Yankee Doodle Dandy*
1943 Paul Lukas *Watch on the Rhine*
1944 Bing Crosby *Going My Way*
1945 Ray Milland *The Lost Weekend*
1946 Fredric March *The Best Years of Our Lives*
1947 Ronald Colman *A Double Life*
1948 Laurence Olivier *Hamlet*
1949 Broderick Crawford *All the King's Men*

BEST ACTRESS

1940 Ginger Rogers *Kitty Foyle*
1941 Joan Fontaine *Suspicion*
1942 Greer Garson *Mrs Miniver*
1943 Jennifer Jones *The Song of Bernadette*
1944 Ingrid Bergman *Gaslight*
1945 Joan Crawford *Mildred Pierce*
1946 Olivia de Havilland *To Each His Own*
1947 Loretta Young *The Farmer's Daughter*
1948 Jane Wyman *Johnny Belinda*
1949 Olivia de Havilland *The Heiress*

BEST DIRECTOR

1940 John Ford *The Grapes of Wrath*
1941 John Ford *How Green Was My Valley*
1942 William Wyler *Mrs Miniver*
1943 Michael Curtiz *Casablanca*
1944 Leo McCarey *Going My Way*
1945 Billy Wilder *The Lost Weekend*
1946 William Wyler *The Best Years of Our Lives*
1947 Elia Kazan *Gentleman's Agreement*
1948 John Huston *The Treasure of the Sierra Madre*
1949 Joseph L. Mankiewicz *A Letter to Three Wives*

BEST PICTURE

1940 *Rebecca*
1941 *How Green Was My Valley*
1942 *Mrs Miniver*
1943 *Casablanca*
1944 *Going My Way*
1945 *The Lost Weekend*
1946 *The Best Years of Our Lives*
1947 *Gentleman's Agreement*
1948 *Hamlet*
1949 *All the King's Men*

NOBEL PRIZES

The Nobel Prizes are an international award granted in the fields of literature, physics, chemistry, physiology or medicine, and peace. The first prizes were awarded in 1901 and funded by the money left in the will of the Swedish inventor Alfred Nobel (1833–96), who gave the world dynamite.

PRIZES FOR LITERATURE

1940–1943 *No awards*
1944 Johannes Jensen (Danish) for poetry and fiction
1945 Gabriela Mistral (Chilean) for poetry
1946 Hermann Hesse (German) for fiction, poetry and essays
1947 André Gide (French) for fiction
1948 T.S. Eliot (British) for poetry, essays and drama
1949 William Faulkner (American) for fiction (Award delayed until 1950.)

PRIZES FOR PEACE

1940–1943 *No awards*
1944 The International Red Cross for doing relief work during World War II
1945 Cordell Hull (American) for peace efforts as secretary of state
1946 John R. Mott (American) for YMCA work and for aiding displaced persons, and Emily Greene Balch (American) for work with the Women's International League for Peace and Freedom
1947 The Friends Service Council and the American Friends Service Committee for humanitarian work
1948 *No award*
1949 John Boyd Orr (British) for directing the United Nations Food and Agriculture Organization

PRIZES FOR PHYSICS

1940–1942 *No awards*
1943 Otto Stern (American) for discovering the molecular beam method of studying the atom
1944 Isidor Isaac Rabi (American) for recording the magnetic properties of atomic nuclei
1945 Wolfgang Pauli (Austrian) for discovering the exclusion principle (Pauli principle) of electrons
1946 Percy William Bridgman (American) for his work in the field of very high pressures
1947 Sir Edward Appleton (British) for exploring the ionosphere
1948 Patrick Blackett (British) for his discoveries in cosmic radiation
1949 Hideki Yukawa (Japanese) for predicting the existence of elementary particles called mesons

PRIZES FOR CHEMISTRY

1940–1942 *No awards*
1943 Georg von Hevesy (Hungarian) for using isotopes as indicators in chemistry
1944 Otto Hahn (German) for discoveries in fission
1945 Artturi Virtanen (Finnish) for inventing new methods in agricultural biochemistry
1946 James B. Sumner (American) for discovering that enzymes can be crystallized; and Wendell M. Stanley and John H. Northrop (American) for preparing pure enzymes and virus proteins
1947 Sir Robert Robinson (British) for research on biologically significant plant substances
1948 Arne Tiselius (Swedish) for discoveries on the nature of serum proteins
1949 William Francis Giauque (American) for studying reactions to extreme cold

PRIZES FOR PHYSIOLOGY OR MEDICINE

1940–1942 *No awards*
1943 Henrik Dam (Danish) for discovering vitamin K and Edward Doisy (American) for synthesizing it
1944 Joseph Erlanger and Herbert Gasser (American) for work on single nerve fibres
1945 Alexander Fleming (British) for discovering penicillin, and Howard Florey and Ernst Chain (British) for developing its use as an antibiotic
1946 Hermann Joseph Muller (American) for discovering that X-rays can produce mutations
1947 Carl and Gerty Cori (American) for their work on insulin; and Bernardo Houssay (Argentine) for studying the pancreas and the pituitary gland
1948 Paul Muller (Swiss) for discovering the insect-killing properties of DDT
1949 Walter Hess (Swiss) for discovering how certain parts of the brain control organs of the body; and Antonio Moniz (Portuguese) for originating prefrontal lobotomy

U.S. PRESIDENTS

1933–1945 President Franklin Delano Roosevelt, *Democrat*
1933–1941 Vice President John N. Garner; 1941–1945 Vice President Henry A. Wallace; 1945 Vice President Harry S. Truman
1945–1953 President Harry S. Truman, *Democrat*
1949–1953 Vice President Alben W. Barkley

SITES OF THE OLYMPIC GAMES

1940 SUMMER *Not held*
WINTER *Not held*
1944 SUMMER *Not held*
WINTER *Not held*
1948 SUMMER London, England
WINTER St Moritz, Switzerland

INDIANAPOLIS 500

1940 Wilbur Shaw
1941 Mauri Rose in relief of Floyd Davis
1942-1945 *No race held*
1946 George Robson
1947 Mauri Rose
1948 Mauri Rose
1949 Bill Holland

KENTUCKY DERBY

1940 Gallahadion
1941 Whirlaway
1942 Shut Out
1943 Count Fleet
1944 Pensive
1945 Hoop, Jr.
1946 Assault
1947 Jet Pilot
1948 Citation
1949 Ponder

NBA CHAMPIONS

1947 Philadelphia Warriors defeat Chicago Stags
1948 Baltimore Bullets defeat Philadelphia Warriors
1949 Minneapolis Lakers defeat Washington Capitals

WORLD SERIES CHAMPIONS

1940 Cincinnati Reds defeat Detroit Tigers
1941 New York Yankees defeat Brooklyn Dodgers
1942 St. Louis Cardinals defeat New York Yankees
1943 New York Yankees defeat St. Louis Cardinals
1944 St. Louis Cardinals defeat St. Louis Browns
1945 Detroit Tigers defeat Chicago Cubs
1946 St. Louis Cardinals defeat Boston Red Sox
1947 New York Yankees defeat Brooklyn Dodgers
1948 Cleveland Indians defeat Boston Braves
1949 New York Yankees defeat Brooklyn Dodgers

A

Abelson, Philip H., 9
abortion, 55
Actor's Studio, 48
Adidas, 55
Admiral Graf Spee, 22
Agee, James, 12
Aiken, Howard H., 35
aircraft
  ejector seat, 45
  experimental, 12
  Flying Dutchman, 60
  Flying Wing, 55
  He-280, 20
  Lancaster bombers, 31
  Me-262 jets,
  (Messerschmitts), 20,
  26
  Sikorsky XR-2, 27
  Spruce Goose, 46, 47
  twin-engine fighter, 12,
  20
Albania
  Greek civil war, 44
Anouilh, Jean, 27
antibiotics
  chloramphenicol, 49
  penicillin, 9
Anzio, battle of, 17
apartheid, 52
Arab-Israeli War, 52, 53,
58
Arab League, 35
architecture
  Glass House, 60
Ardennes, battle of, 18
Argentina
  Péron, 42
Arnhem, battle of, 18
Arnold, Kenneth, 48
Atlantic Charter, 10, 12
atomic power
  bombs, 36, 38, 40, 41
  test, 36, 39, 42, 43, 44
atoms
  nuclear structure, 55
  pions, 49
Attlee, Clement, 8
Auschwitz, 36, 37
Austria
  annexed, 14, 15
Axis Powers, 16, 17, 28

B

baby boom, 46, 50
Back, Frank, 45
Bacon, Francis, 35
Bardeen, John, 50
Barrault, Jean-Louis, 39
baseball
  Babe Ruth dies, 52
  Brooklyn Dodgers, 49,
  50
  New York Yankees, 12
  Robinson, Jackie, 46,
  49, 50
Bataan death march, 24
Battle of Britain, 7, 20
Beauvoir, de Simone, 45,
59
Belgium
  annexed, 7
  Brussels liberated, 32
Belgrade
  occupied, 10
Benelux, 49
Ben-Gurion, David, 53
Bennet, Joan, 57

Bergman, Ingrid, 26, 27,
57
Berlin
  airlift, 52, 58, 61
  blockade, 58
  Soviets, 54
  WWII, 17, 32, 36
Berlin, Irving, 26
bikini, 42, 45
Bikini Atoll, 42, 43
Bizmarck, battleship, 10,
22
Blankers-Koen, Fanny, 55
blender, first electric, 50
Bletchly Park, 31
Blitz, 8, 13
Blitzkrieg, 8, 13, 20, 34
Bogart, Humphrey, 26, 27
Bonnard, Pierre, 46
Borglum, Gutzon, 13
Bourke-White, Margaret,
38
Brando, Marlon, 48, 49
Brandt, Bill, 53
Brattain, Walter, 50
Brecht, Bertolt, 12
Breton Woods
  Conference, 33
Britain
  Battle of, 20
  Churchill, PM, 7, 8
  Coventry, 8, 20
  declares war, 14
  Dunkirk, 7
  Greek civil war, 44
  Indian independence,
  44, 46
  London bombed, 8, 13,
  20, 34
  Malaysian campaign, 52,
  53
  National Health
  Service, 52, 54
  Olympic Games,
  London, 52
  Palestine, 47
Broz, Joseph, *see* Tito
Bruneval, battle of, 18
Buchenwald, 38
Bulgaria
  Greek civil war, 44
Bulge, battle of the, 39
Burma
  WWII, 19

C

calculator, mechanical, 35,
60
Camus, Albert, 27
can, self-heating, 27
Cape Matapan, 22
Capone, Al, 46, 49
carbon-14 dating, 47
Carver, George
  Washington, 28
Casablanca, 26, 27
Casablanca Agreement,
30, 31
Chamberlain, Neville, 8,
9
Chandler, Raymond,
35
Chaplin, Charlie, 7, 9
Chiang Kai-shek, 38, 54,
59
China
  Chiang Kai-shek, 38,
  54, 59

civil war, 36, 38, 46, 52,
54, 58, 59
  Manchuria, 38
  Mao, 38, 59
  People's Republic, 58
  Shanghai, 37, 58
  Taiwan, 59
chloramphenicol, 49
Churchill, Winston
  Casablanca Agreement,
  30, 31
  Conservative Party, 9
  Iron Curtain, 42, 44
  Potsdam, 36, 38
  Prime Minister, 7, 8
  Tehran, 28
  WWII, 26, 28
  Yalta, 36, 37
Citizen Kane, 12
clock, atomic, 54
Coeliac disease, 9
Cold War
  Iron Curtain, 42
Colossus, 31
Cominform
  Yugoslavia expelled, 52
computer
  bug, 38
  ENIAC, 39, 42
  first, 28, 36
Congress of Racial
  Equality (CORE), 27
Cooper, Gary, 57
Coral Sea, battle of, 23
Corregidor, battle of, 19,
37
Coryell, Charles, D., 39
Coutances, battle of, 18
Coventry, 8, 20
Crab Nebula, 50
Crawford, Cheryl, 48
Crete
  Operation Mercury, 16
Crosby, Bing, 27
Cry, The Beloved Country,
53
cybernetics, 55
Czechoslovakia
  annexed, 14, 15
  Communists coup, 52,
  53

D

Dachau, 37
Dacron, *see* polyester
  fiber
Dambusters, 20, 28
Dassler, Adolf, 55
D-Day, 18, 32
Dead Sea Scrolls, 50
death camps, 36, 37, 38
Declaration of Human
  Rights, 52
De Gaulle, Charles
  England, 7
  Free French, 8
  Paris, 33, 34
  resigns presidency, 42,
  44
Denmark
  annexed, 7, 14
  Iceland, 34
De Valera, Eamon, 52
Dewey, Thomas E., 55
Dickson, J.T., 13
Dieppe, battle of, 18
Dior, Christian, 46, 47
Doolittle, James, 21

draft, military lottery,
  U.S., 7
Dresden, 36, 37
Dunkirk, 7, 14

E

Egypt
  Arab-Israeli War, 52,
  53
Eisenhower, Dwight D.,
  35
Eisenstein, Sergei, 52
El Alamein, battle of, 16,
  24
elements
  berkelium, 60
  californium, 60
  neptunium, 9
  plutonium, 9
  promethium, 39
Eliot, T.S., 52
Enola Gay, 40
espresso, 42, 45
Eugenic Protection Law,
  55
Evans, Walker, 12
Existentialism
  Sartre, 31
Eysenck, Hans, 50

F

Falaise Pocket, battle of,
  18
Farmer, James, 27
Fermi, Enrico, 27
Feynman, Richard, 55
Fields, W.C., 42
Final Solution, 24, 26, 37
Finland
  Winter War, 7, 8
Fitzgerald, Francis Scott,
  8
Fleming, Sir Alexander,
  39
Flying Dutchman, 60
foods, convenience, 60
For Whom the Bell Tolls, 8,
  57
Ford, Henry, 46, 50
Ford, John, 57
France
  D-Day, 18, 32
  defeat, 7, 8
  De Gaulle, 7, 8, 33, 34,
  42, 44
  Free French, 8
  Indochinese War, 42,
  44
  liberated, 33, 34
  Pétain, 8
  Vichy, 24, 27
Frank, Anne, 46, 49
Frankfurter Zeitung, 31
Free French
  De Gaulle, 8, 33
French Indochinese War
  Haiphong, 42

G

Gandhi, Mahatma, 52, 55
Gasperi, Alcide de, 44
George, David Lloyd, 38
Germany
  Berlin Airlift, 52, 58, 61

Blitzkrieg, 8, 20
  Communist
  Democratic Republic,
  58, 59
  Federal Republic of
  Germany, 58, 59
  Luftwaffe, 14, 16
  Nazi Party, 15
  Nuremburg, 14, 15
  surrender, 36
G.I. Bill of Rights, 32, 48
Giacometti, Alberto, 45
Gibson, Guy, 31
Glendenin, Lawrence E.,
  39
Gloster Meteor, 12
Greece
  civil war, 42, 44, 58
  defeat, 10
  German invasion, 16
  Italian invasion, 7
  WWII, 16
Guam, battle for, 19
gypsies
  Auschwitz, 37

H

Hague, The
  International Court of
  Justice, 38
Haiphong, 42
Hale, George E., 53
hamburger, 7
Hammerstein, Oscar, 31
Hemingway, Ernest, 8, 57
Heyerdahl, Thor, 55
Hiroshima, 21, 36, 40, 41
Hitchcock, Alfred, 56
Hitler, Adolf,
  assassination attempt,
  32, 33
  Final Solution, 24
  suicide, 36, 37
Ho Chi Minh, 38, 42
Hofmann, Albert, 28, 31
Holland
  annexed, 7, 14
  Indonesia, 52, 54, 59
  Juliana succeeds, 54
  Wilhelmina abdicates,
  52, 54
Hollywood, 49, 56, 57
Holocaust, 36, 37, 49
Hong Kong, battle of, 19
Hope, Bob, 27
Hopper, Grace Murray,
  38
Hughes, Howard, 46, 47
human rights
  Declaration of Human
  Rights, 52, 54
  European Court of
  Human Rights, 59
Hynkel, Adenoid, 9

I

ice hockey, 7
Iceland, 32, 34
India
  civil disorder, 26, 44
  Gandhi assassinated,
  52, 55
  independence, 46
  Kashmir, 60
  partition, 46, 47

war with Pakistan, 58,
  60
Indonesia, 36, 38, 52, 58,
  59
insecticide, 12
International Court of
  Justice, 38
International Monetary
  Fund, 32, 33
Iraq
  Arab-Israeli War, 52,
  53
Ireland
  de Valera, PM, 52
Iron Curtain, 42, 44
Israel
  Ben-Gurion, PM, 53
  invaded, 52
  Mandate ends, 53
  recognized, 53
  State proclaimed, 52
  Weizmann, 53
Italy
  Axis Alliance, 7
  Dodecanese Islands, 44
  Exposizione Universale
  di Roma, 8
  invasion of Greece, 7
  Mussolini assassinated,
  36, 37
  Palazzo della Civilita del
  Lavoro, 8
  Umberto II exiled, 44
  votes for republic, 42
  women vote, 44
  WWII, 7, 17, 28, 31
Iwo Jima, 19, 37

J

Japan
  Axis Alliance, 7
  kamikaze, 21
  Neutrality Pact, 10
  Pearl Harbor, 10, 11,
  19, 21
  surrenders, 36, 38
  Tokyo, bombed, 21, 37
jeep, 9
Jensen, Hans, 54
Jews
  Auschwitz, 36
  Final Solution, 24, 26,
  36
  Holocaust, 36
  Warsaw Ghetto, 27
  yellow star, 11
Johnson, Amy, 11
Johnson, John Harold, 27
Johnson, Philip, 60
Jordan
  Arab-Israeli War, 52,
  53
Joyce, James, 12
Juliana, Queen of
  Holland, 54

K

kamikaze, 21
Katyn Forest massacre,
  30, 31
Kawabe, Torashiro, 38
Kazan, Elia, 48
Kazantzakis, Nikos, 44
Keynes, John Maynard, 45
Kharkov, battle of, 17
kidney dialysis, 31

Kiev
occupied, 10
Kinsey, Alfred, 52
Klee, Paul, 7
Kolff, Willem J., 31
Kramer, Jack, 46
Kuiper, Gerard P., 54, 60
Kuomintang, 58
Kursk, battle of, 17

L

Land, Edwin H., 50
Landsteiner, Karl, 9
Lang, Fritz, 57
Lascaux, 8
Lebanon
Arab-Israeli War, 52, 53
Lend-Lease Bill, 10, 25
Leningrad
besieged, 17, 28
Les Enfants du Paradis, 36, 39
Let Us Now Praise Famous Men, 12
Levine, Philip, 9
Lewis, Robert, 48
Leyte Gulf, battle of, 19, 23, 35
Libby, Willard F., 47
Lie, Trygve, 42
London
Blitz, 10, 13, 32, 34
Lorca, Federico, 44
LSD, 28, 31
Ludendorf Bridge, battle of, 36
Luftwaffe, 14, 20, 34
Luzon, battle of, 19

M

MacArthur, Douglas, 32, 35
MacMurray, Fred, 35
Mailer, Norman, 53
Malan, Douglas, 53
Malaysia
Anti-British compaign, 53
Communists, 52
Malayan Races Liberation Army (MRLA), 53
WWII, 19
Mao Zedong, 38, 58, 59
Marinsky, J.A., 39
Mars, 54
Marshall, George, 46, 47, 51
Marshall Plan, 46, 47, 51
Martin, James, 45
Masaryk, Jan, 53
Mayer, Maria Goeppert, 54
McDonald, Richard and Maurice, 9
McMillan, Edwin M., 9
medicine
blood, Rh factor, 9
chloramphenicol, 49
Coeliac disease, 9
penicillin, 9
streptomycin, 34
Messiaen, Olivier, 54
Mestral, George de, 55

Method Acting, *see*
Stanislavski Method
microwave oven, 50
Midway, battle of, 23, 24
Miller, Arthur, 59
Miller, Glenn, 26, 33
Minsk, battle of, 17
Mondrian, Piet, 34
Monte Cassino, battle of, 17
Montgomery, General
El Alamein, 16
Moore, Henry, 10
Mother Courage, 12
Mount Rushmore, 10, 13
Munch, Edvard, 32
Musashi, battleship, 23
Mussolini, Benito
assassinated, 36, 37
WWII, 31
Myrdal, Gunnar, 31

N

Nagasaki, 21, 36, 38, 40, 41
Nazi Party
Final Solution, 24, 26, 36, 37
Nuremburg War Trials, 36, 38
"undesirables," 37
Neptune
Nereid, 60
Netherlands, The
annexed, 7
Indonesia, 36, 38, 52, 58, 59
liberated, 34
royal family, 35
New Guinea
WWII, 19, 35
New Look, The, 46, 47
Normany invasion, see
D-Day
North Africa
WWII, 16, 51
North American Treaty
Organization (NATO), 58, 59
North Korea, 52
Norway
annexed, 14
nuclear bomb
Hiroshima, 21, 36, 38
Nagasaki, 21, 36, 38
tested, 36, 39, 42, 43, 44
nuclear power
reactor, 27
Nuremburg
rally, 14, 15
Trials, 36, 38

O

Okinawa, battle of, 19, 36, 37
Olivier, Lawrence, 39
Olympic Games
cancelled, 8, 33
London, 52, 55
St. Moritz, 52, 53, 55
Operation Cerberus, 22
Oppenheimer, Robert, 39
orange juice, freeze-dried, 13

Organization of American
States (OAS), 53
Orwell, George, 39, 59
Ossius, Frederick J., 50
Oxfam, 27

P

Pakistan
Kashmir, 60
partition, 46, 47
war with India, 60
Palestine
Arab League, 35
Mandate ends, 53
U.N. partition plan, 46, 47
paper chromatography, 34
Paris
bohemian, 42, 45
liberated, 32, 33, 34
occupation, 7, 8
Paton, Alan, 53
Patton, George S., 39
Pauling, Linus, 58, 60
Pearl Harbor, 10, 11, 19, 21
Peenemunde, battle of, 20
penicillin, 9, 39
Péron, Eva, 44
Péron, Juan, 42, 44
Philippines
independent, 42, 44
WWII, 19, 23, 32, 35, 37, 38
Piccard, Auguste, 54
pion, 49
Planned Parenthood, 55
Plymouth, 8
Poland
annexed, 14
Warsaw uprising, 17
Polaroid, 50
Pollack, Jackson, 39
polyester fiber, 13, 34
Porter, Archer, J.P., 34
Potsdam Conference, 36, 38
Pound, Ezra, 54
Powell, Cecil, 49
psychology
Personality Theory, 50

Q

Quebec Plan, 31
quinine, 34

R

race relations, U.S.
Black Boy, 38
CORE, 27
Robinson, Jackie, 46, 49, 50
Zoot riots, 31
radar signals, 39
Réard, Louis, 45
records, long-playing, 54
Reichstag, 15
Remagen, battle of, 18
Rhine crossing, 18, 36
Robinson, Edward G., 35

Robinson, Jackie, 46, 49, 50
Rockefeller, John D., Jr., 46
Rockefeller, Nelson A., 45
rocket
V-2, 27, 32
WAC Corporal, 60
Rogers, Richard, 31
Rommel, Erwin, 9, 13
Afrika Korps, 16
Roosevelt, Eleanor, 54
Roosevelt, Franklin D.
Atlantic Charter, 12
Casablanca, 30
dies, 36, 37, 39
fourth term, 32
Tehran, 28, 31
third term, 7
Yalta, 36, 37
Royal Air Force (RAF), 18, 20, 24, 31
Ruth, Babe, 52, 55

S

Saipan, battle of, 19
Salerno, battle of, 17
Sanger, Margaret, 55
Sartre, Jean-Paul, 31, 39, 45
Schockley, William, 50
SCUBA, 31
Seaborg, Glenn T., 9, 60
Sevastopol, battle of, 17
Seyfert, Carl K., 31
Shostakovich, Dmitri, 12
Sicily, landings, 17, 28, 31
sickle cell anemia, 58, 60
Sinatra, Frank, 29
Singapore
WWII, 19, 24, 26
skydiving, 55
Smuts, Jan, 52
Smyth, Dame Ethel Mary, 33
Snead, Sam, 58
sound barrier, 46, 48, 49
South Africa
apartheid, 52
Smuts ousted, 52
Soviet Union
atomic bomb testing, 58, 59
Cominform, 52, 54
Israel recognized, 53
pact with China, 10
Winter War Truce, 7, 8
WWII, 17
spam, 10, 12
Spencer, Percy LeBaron, 50
Spock, Benjamin, 50
Stalin, Josef
Potsdam, 36, 38
Tehran, 28, 31
Yalta, 36, 37
Yugoslavia, 54
Stalingrad, battle of, 17
Stanislavski Method, 48
Stanwyck, Barbara, 35
Stauffenberg, Claus von, 32, 33
streptomycin, 34
Sukarno, Ahmed, 54, 59
Sullivan, W.N., 12

Sweeney, Charles, 21
Synge, Richard, 34
Syria
Arab-Israeli War, 52, 53

T

T-shirt, 27
Tanzania
Serengeti, 9
Taranto, battle of, 22
Tarawa, battle of, 19
Tashin, Col., 24
Tehran Conference, 28, 31
telescope, Hale, 53
television, color, 9
Terylene, see polyester fiber
The Second Sex, 59
Thondup, Llhamo, 8
Tibbets, Paul, 21, 38
Tibet
Dalai Lama, 8
Tippett, Michael, 35
tires, tubeless, 54
Tito, Josip, 54
Tobruk, battle of, 16
Tokyo, bombed, 21
Torch landings, 16
transistor, invented, 50
Trotsky, Leon, 7, 8
Truman, Harry
Doctrine, 46, 47
Potsdam, 36, 38
President, 37, 55

U

U-boats, 28, 31
Umberto II, King of Italy, 44
Unidentified Flying
Objects (UFO's), 48
United Nations
Declaration of Human
Rights, 52, 54
declared, 24, 26
founded, 36, 38
Lie, Trygve, 42
London session, 42
partition of Palestine, 46
San Francisco confer-ence, 37
United Nations General
Assembly
New York City, 42
United States
Berlin Airlift, 52, 58, 61
D-Day, 18, 32
G.I. Bill of Rights, 32, 48
House Un-American
Activities Committee, 49
Israel recognized, 53
Lend-Lease Bill, 10
Marshall Plan, 46, 47, 51
Pearl Harbor, 10, 11, 19, 21
race relations, 27, 31
USAF, 20
United States Air Force
(USAF), 20

V

Valentin, Leo, 55
VE Day, 36, 38
Vergeltungswaffen, 20
Vichy, 24, 27
Victor Emmanuel, King
dismisses Mussolini, 31
Vietnam
emperor deposed, 38
Ho Chi Minh, 38, 42
republic, 38, 42, 44
Vrzanova, Aja, 53

W

Waksman, Selman, 34
Wallis, Barnes, 31
Wannsee Conference, 26
Warsaw
city uprising, 33
Ghetto, 27
Ghetto uprising, 17, 28
Soviets, 36
Weizmann, Chaim, 53
Welles, Orson, 12, 59
Whinfield, John, 34
Whitfield, J.R., 13
Wiener, Norbert, 55
Wilder, Billy, 35
Wilhelmina, Queen, 52, 54
Williams, Tennessee, 46, 48, 49
Williams, William Carlos, 45
Wilson, Edmund, 45
Wimbledon
Championships, 46
Winter War
truce, 8
women
abortion, 55
Army Corps, U.S., 35
The Second Sex, 59
voting, 44
Women's Liberation
Movement, 59
working, 28, 29
Woolf, Virginia, 10, 13
World Bank, 32, 33
Wright, Richard, 38
Wyeth, Andrew, 54

Y

Yalta Conference, 36
Yamato, battleship, 23
Yeager, Chuck, 46, 48, 49
Yugoslavia
Belgrade occupied, 10
Cominform, 52, 54
German invasion, 16
Greek civil war, 44
WWII, 16

Z

zoom lens, 45
Zoot riots, 31
Zorba the Greek, 44